NEW MEXICO FOOD TRAILS

Trainwreck
IPA

Hoppy
Hophead

Wet Hop
Hazardous
IPA

Irish
Red

New Mexico Food Trails

A Road Tripper's Guide
to Hot Chile, Cold Brews,
and Classic Dishes from
the Land of Enchantment

CAROLYN GRAHAM

University of New Mexico Press • Albuquerque

ISBN 978-0-8263-6247-6 (paper)
ISBN 978-0-8263-6248-3 (electronic)

Library of Congress Control Number: 2021931612

Cover photo and imagae on page vi: Courtesy
of Douglas K. Hill, www.hillphoto.com

Map by Mindy Basinger Hill

Composed in Minion Pro and Gotham

TO MOM AND DAD

For giving me a happy and food-filled New Mexico childhood

that led me to writing a travel guide rather than a tell-all

Contents

Introduction New Mexico Food Trails
The Start of a Delicious Road Trip

The main ingredient in this book—and in every person who produced every dish and drink in it—is passion. It's passion for the craft of cuisine, for finding fresh ways of combining ingredients, for putting something new in the glass or on the plate. It's passion for sharing something, for serving something that will make people happy. The folks who run or work at New Mexico's wonderful eateries and drinkeries want to make people feel welcome, full, and, on some level, loved.

For those of us lucky enough to be their guests, there is joy in knowing that the plate set before us was the brainchild of someone, the result of an entrepreneurial spark, and that the creator wants us to love it as much as they do.

I am not a food critic. My training is as a journalist, and I discovered a passion for food and food writing later in life. I grew up in Las Cruces, a second-generation New Mexican. My dad was born and raised in the chile heartland of the United States, the tiny farming village of Hatch, which has become synonymous with the state's most famous pepper. My dad's dad was a cook, a native Louisianan who had traveled quite a bit with his family before settling in Hatch, where he opened Short's Café. He served Hatch farmers and farmhands, and everyone else in town. The family story is that he opened a satellite café in the 1930s to serve workers who were building Caballo Dam, near modern-day Truth or Consequences and Elephant Butte.

I never got to meet my grandfather, but I glimpse a bit of his spirit in the people whose livelihoods revolve around New Mexico cuisine. Everyone believes their home state is full of good things to eat, but New Mexicans know that our food is truly special. The state's mix of cultures and landscapes creates a heartiness that shines through in its cuisine, whether it's a spicy chile relleno or a crisp viognier.

This guide is an exploration of New Mexico's classic and popular flavors

Green chile cheeseburgers and other classic New Mexican dishes come in many forms throughout the state.

and ingredients and dishes that have inspired our state's talented hands to put their own spins on them. Each stop along the way reflects its maker's vision in a different way.

The Spice of Life

New Mexico's signature dishes and beverages have evolved due to a variety of factors, and they boast many regional distinctions. New Mexico is practically a square, about 370 miles long and 340 miles wide, and covers three topographic zones: Rocky Mountain, Plains, and Intermountain Plateau. So chile grows differently in the Rio Grande Valley than it does in the hills of Chimayó, which sits at the foot of the Sangre de Cristos. The terroir of the vineyards in Lordsburg is different than that of Dixon. The influences of the people who settled near Taos—where Spaniards, Mexicans, and Puebloans were the primary populations—are different than those of settlers around Carlsbad, where the Dust Bowl, homesteading, and other factors pushed people westward. Las Cruces is close to the borderlands of both Mexico and Texas, so its people have a different story than those in the Four Corners, where the Diné (Navajos) lived hundreds of years before Europeans arrived.

What came of all that migration, immigration, and settling? Over the centuries, chile and grapes were planted, cows and sheep were grazed, and corn, beans, and squash—known by the Puebloans as the Three Sisters—formed the base of this area's food pyramid.

Over time, a cuisine that could be grown and sown here, based on regional palates and influences, has evolved into foods and drinks that are sometimes about convenience (breakfast burritos) and sometimes about religion (wine), agriculture (red or green?), fellowship (diners), or celebration (spirits).

How to Use This Guide

Go ahead: Spill some green chile on this book. It is here to help you plan a journey, discover a new dish or eatery, or remember why you loved a place you visited. You can use it to create a food-focused getaway or pull it out when you're in an unfamiliar place.

Sometimes it's about the food; sometimes it's about the establishment. And when those two come together, it's magical. And while this book is largely focused on where and how to enjoy New Mexico's most famous foods and beverages, I've tucked in a few surprises and helpful tips that go beyond the burgers and enchiladas. I've also called out a few "Top Picks" in each chapter.

For the most part, I selected the places in this guidebook, based on my

New Mexico
Cities and Towns

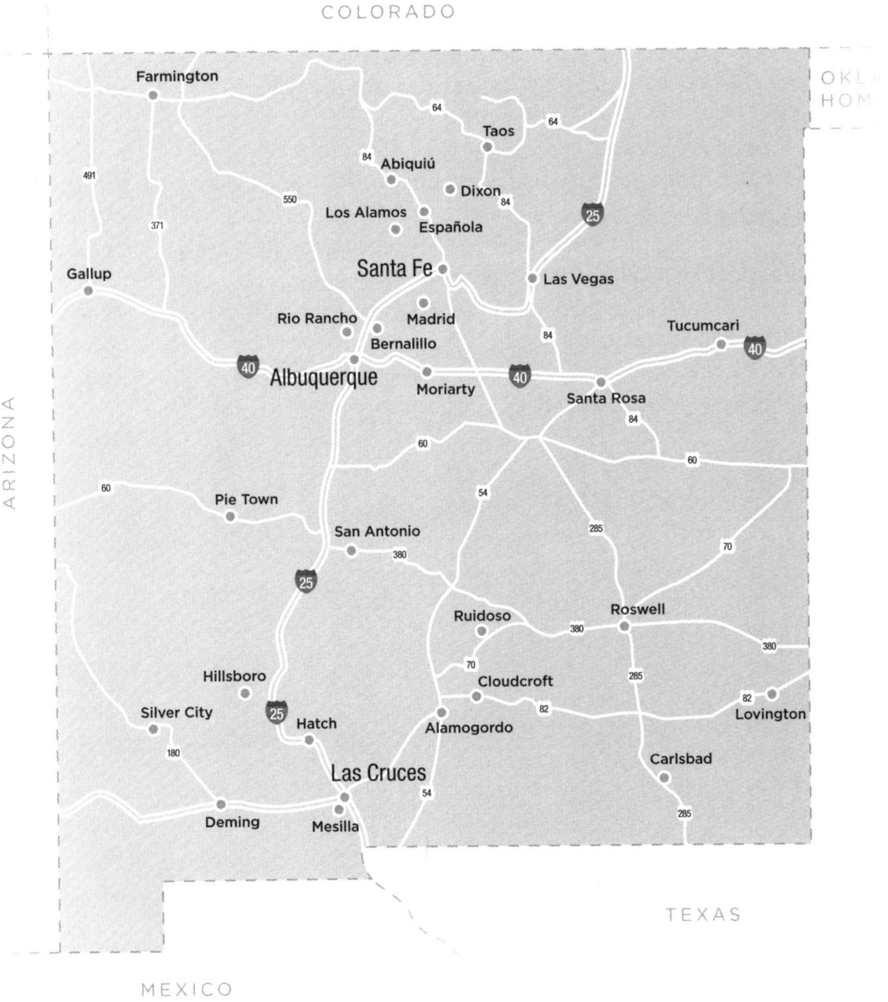

COLORADO

OKLA
HOM

Farmington

64

Taos

64

84

Abiquiú

Dixon

Los Alamos

84

550

Española

371

Santa Fe

Las Vegas

Gallup

Rio Rancho

Madrid

Tucumcari

Bernalillo

84

40

Albuquerque

Moriarty

40

Santa Rosa

84

60

60

Pie Town

54

60

San Antonio

285

70

380

25

Ruidoso

Roswell

380

380

70

Hillsboro

Cloudcroft

285

82

Silver City

25

Hatch

82

Lovington

180

Alamogordo

Carlsbad

Las Cruces

54

Deming

Mesilla

285

ARIZONA

TEXAS

MEXICO

experiences, for one or a combination of these reasons: the quality of the food, interactions with the people, history, or significance in the state.

Because this is a guidebook mostly about burger joints and local eateries, the price range is pretty consistent; the typical plate of enchiladas or a green chile cheeseburger will run you between $10 and $15. In Santa Fe, expect to pay about 50 percent more than that, especially if you're dining on the plaza. I've noted places that are good for cheap eats as well as the ones where "tourist pricing" is in effect.

As with every guidebook, the specifics about these places can change on a dime. And the covid pandemic has forced unexpected changes across the board, from hours of operation and menu tweaks to closings and relocations. Also remember that small rural establishments might not keep consistent hours, and be patient with the mom-and-pop burger restaurant that had to close so that Mom and Pop could attend a wedding. Call ahead and confirm before you make the drive. Lastly, be sure to appreciate the heart, heritage, and history wrapped up in what is on your plate or in your glass.

May your chile be hot and your beer cold. *Buen provecho.*

1 Our History Is Delicious

Take a look at your plate. Here's where your taste buds will tell you what a history book cannot. This amalgam of flavors—whether fried, dried, stewed, boiled, fermented, or raw right out of the field—is the key to our past and what makes modern-day New Mexican foods unique. To experience the state's cuisine is to taste the complex and brilliant end result of hundreds of years of culture, tradition, and agriculture that mix Puebloan, Spanish, Mexican, and Anglo influences with a dash of Middle Eastern and Asian thrown in. The following is but a slice of that history, with the hope that it will kick you out onto a trail to sip and nibble your way through the state.

Bevvies to Beans

New Mexico's wine industry has had a bumpy ride. Franciscan monks from Spain who were imposing Catholicism on the Native population in the West during the seventeenth century were also violating Spanish laws: They were planting wine grapes from smuggled vines. To maintain sovereignty over its wine-making and exporting industry, the Spanish government had declared that Spanish grapes could grow only on Spanish soil. But the monks needed wine for sacramental purposes, and the long trip across the oceans and deserts left Spanish-made wine hard to swallow, even for communion or other official purposes.

The first mission grapes were planted near Socorro in 1629. Ultimately the vineyards expanded and did pretty well in New Mexico, until Prohibition and devastating floods killed off a lot of grapes. Slowly but surely, enterprising New Mexicans brought back the vineyards. Sweet wines were our thing a few decades ago, until winemakers began branching out to meet the demand for more complex, European-style wines that pair with food, such as cabernet sauvignon, syrah, mourvedre, and tempranillo.

So if you've tried New Mexico wines in the past, it's time to take another sip. The state is now home to more than fifty wineries, scattered from north to south, making award-winning wines and providing beautiful spaces to sit in and sip. The New Mexico Wine and Grape Growers Association maintains a wine trail and offers information about special events at nmwine.com.

Another New Mexico sip with a history is chocolate, which, in the form of a hot beverage, seems to awaken something primal in human beings. The warmth seeps into the chest and wraps around the heart, and that satisfyingly sweet and nutty taste evokes an irrepressible smile. Maybe that's because the chocolate sipping experience reaches deep into human history, forming a sensory connection between us and our ancestors.

As it was in the past, making and drinking liquid chocolate is also about geographic ritual and tradition. The British enjoy their afternoon teatime, the Italians prize their espresso, but drinking chocolate is uniquely of the Americas. Analysis of residues inside ancient vessels found at Chaco Culture National Historical Park, a site of human occupation that dates to the

900s B.C., shows that Native peoples in what would become New Mexico were consuming cacao beans at least one thousand years ago. The beans from cacao plants, which tend to grow near the equator, were used for spiritual and ceremonial purposes among the Mayans and the Aztecs. Trading routes brought them north, and Spanish explorers partook in chocolate-sipping rituals as they moved along El Camino Real, the route that connected Mexico City to Spanish territories in the north, during the eighteenth and nineteenth centuries.

Modern-day chocoholics partake in some of the same flavors and textures that our forebears did, reminding us that food has always had a powerful hold over people. You can follow the early explorers' footsteps on the New Mexico Tourism Department's Chocolate Trail odyssey, which offers a guide to bean-to-bar chocolatiers, elixir makers, and other chocolate-centric stops, such as Kakawa Chocolate House in Santa Fe. Following the trail is the ideal way to warm up and connect with the past.

Cacao, of course, is far from New Mexico's best-known bean. Despite being mocked as the "musical fruit," beans have been important to human survival for thousands of years. Several varieties of beans arrived from Peru and Mexico via trading routes in the mid-sixteenth century, and soon the lowly frijole was elevated to an essential element in Pueblo diets and ceremonies.

During World War II, New Mexico helped feed soldiers with its abundant pinto bean crops, much of which came from the Estancia Valley in the central part of the state before a hard-hitting drought stifled production. The pinto bean became New Mexico's official state vegetable in 1965 and remains abundant among our farmlands. Often cooked until gloopy, but packed with protein, beans bind New Mexican cuisine at its core, whether they're filling out

combination plates, refried or whole, or serving as the glue that holds our burritos in their proper shape. The bespeckled pinto bean even starred in the 1988 film *The Milagro Beanfield War*, about a farmer and townsfolk in the fictional New Mexico town of Milagro who fight to save a bean field from greedy developers.

Every New Mexican cook has his or her own bean recipe, and many put on a pot when they rise to make their morning coffee. Some like to throw in bacon or ham, while purists stick with just stock and garlic. Restaurants throughout New Mexico put their own spin on beans too, so don't assume they're just taking up space next to your enchiladas.

Crunch Time

New Mexico is pretty nutty: More than 90 million pounds of pecans and pistachios are grown in the state. And while peanuts technically are not nuts (they're legumes), our southeastern farms produce large crops of them. Another shell-covered native food found throughout New Mexico, thanks to our pine-covered hillsides, is the piñon.

Pecans cropped up in the lower Rio Grande Valley in the early 1900s and have expanded to outpace production in Georgia and Texas. The state exports them raw as well as in the form of candy and as an enhancement in beer, cookies, and other dishes. In the Las Cruces area, the first large-scale plantings were established in the 1930s by Deane Stahmann Farms, and as the trees and production grew, so did other orchards.

Pistachios arrived on the New Mexico scene in the 1980s when the late Thomas McGinn planted an arid stretch of land just north of Alamogordo in the Tularosa Basin. The trees are crazy about desert heat (they originated in ancient Persia) and have thrived here—so much so that the McGinn family erected a giant pistachio statue at

New Mexico's pistachio history is celebrated in Alamogordo at McGinn's Pistachio Tree Ranch, home of the World's Largest Pistachio Nut.

their storefront; it has become a major roadside attraction. Learn more about pistachio history and other trivia by taking the McGinns' fun orchard tour aboard a bright green motorized cart (see page 110).

Piñons, or pine nuts, are produced by the wild piñon pine, which is native to New Mexico and also happens to be the official state tree. The little brown seeds have a hard shell and grow from inside the cone. Every four to seven years, depending on the climate and weather factors, the trees produce crops that are harvested in fall. Inside the shell is a sweet, buttery little kernel that is both flavorful and protein-packed.

Birds, bears, and other critters hoover them up voraciously. For hundreds of years, piñons have also been a dietary and medicinal staple for Mescalero Apache, Diné, and Puebloan peoples. In modern times, the nuts are used in everything from coffee and candles to soups and soaps. In the fall, families still make a ritual out of nut gathering,

heading to the state's forested hills to sit under the trees and picnic as they gather nuts. In the winter, burning piñon wood in fireplaces is New Mexico's signature aroma, signaling that it's time to put out the luminarias (or *farolitos*, as they're known around Santa Fe and Taos) and snuggle up together.

Though peanuts are technically in the lentil and pea family, they act like nuts, smooshing up to pair beautifully with jam and bread. The Portales region is our state's peanut hotbed, which has come into its own since the first crops were planted there in the early 1900s. Peanut growing in New Mexico has had its ups and downs over the past decades, but these days the Valencia peanut, introduced to the region by a local farmer in the 1970s, is a vital part of the area economy. While peanuts don't have the same great marketing as green chile, and a big portion of our crop is shipped to out-of-state distributors, just know that if you're eating peanuts at a ball game, they were probably grown in New Mexico.

If you're more of a corn chip snacker, in this state, you'll want those chips to have a case of the blues. While it has been said that wheat is the staff of life, New Mexico's Puebloans have long believed that corn is also a primary staple. It is also the third pillar of the Three Sisters, the agricultural trilogy honored by the Puebloans that also includes beans and squash. While blue corn has long been dried and ground into flour for breads and other foods, it is also used in ceremonies and is an important symbol among the Pueblo cultures.

Unlike yellow or white corns, the blues tend to be fussy growers, requiring careful cultivation and hand harvesting. And while yellow and white tortillas are the wrappers of choice for most tacos and enchiladas, the blues have a special place in hearts and on menus throughout New Mexico. A number of restaurants—especially in central and northern New Mexico, where the Puebloan influence on our cuisine is strong—feature blue corn tortillas (which don't get as soggy) on their plates. With its nuttier, earthier flavor, blue corn is also used in pancakes, muffins, cookies, pizza crust, chips, and other dishes.

Hot, Hot, Hot

Many of New Mexico's most delightful carb-loaded dishes come out of a humble little *horno* (pronounced "or-NO"). These rounded, aboveground adobe ovens, which dot pueblos and neighborhoods throughout central and northern New Mexico, were introduced here (along with wheat) by the Spaniards, who had been introduced to them by the Moors, a population of Muslims who lived in what is now Spain and Portugal.

The Native population recognized the power of this invention, making it their own and using it to cook breads in small

Outdoor adobe ovens, called *hornos*, dot the northern New Mexico landscape. Photo by Jann Huizenga | istockphoto.com.

and large quantities. Horno-baked breads and pies are readily available at the pueblos and during feast days and other celebrations, so be sure to partake at every opportunity.

If you can't get your bread baked, get it fried, either in the form of flat fry bread, popular at the pueblos, or as sopaipillas, pillowy dough that is ubiquitous throughout New Mexican restaurants.

In the nineteenth century, Native Americans devised fry bread from the meager rations provided by the US government to endure long marches from their lands to reservations, where they did not have access to their customary dietary ingredients. While its history is entangled, fry bread endures as a popular treat at pow-wows and pueblos (see "A Word about Fry Bread" on page 107).

As for sopaipillas, Spaniards most likely introduced this culinary concept to the territory that would become New Mexico. Latin American countries such as Argentina and Peru also have a strong connection to these simple fried dough squares. They offer the deep-fried satisfaction of a churro as well as bubbly pockets that can hold fillings ranging from honey globs to scoops of meat and beans. About them, I have but one question: Why haven't sopaipillas gone national?

At most New Mexican restaurants, sopaipillas are as ubiquitous as forks and napkins. Some diners use them to soak up extra red or green chile left behind after they've polished off an enchilada, while others see them purely as dessert, made for holding honey or a dusting of cinnamon sugar. They might also be used to wrap beef patties for a southwestern variation on a burger, or serve as edible shells for ground beef, beans, and green chile. No matter why you fry them, New Mexicans are grateful that someone had the foresight to put them on a menu, so that baskets of the steaming dough puffs will forever enhance our tables.

Speaking of chile, do you feel that burn? That's generations of cultivation followed by a century of agricultural and market research. It's safe to say that New Mexicans are pod people, and as such, we are the nation's top producer of chile. Our top crop is also a source of state pride and has become fused to our collective soul, which is probably because growing chile is only part of the magic. We've also found the best ways to deliver chile to our taste buds.

Theories about the arrival of the first chiles are hotly debated, but early versions have likely been around since the mid-1500s. Spaniards introduced more modern cultivation techniques, which led to chile proliferation throughout the territory. In the early 1900s, at the New Mexico College of Agriculture and Mechanic Arts in Las Cruces (before it became New Mexico State University), horticulturist Fabián García developed chile varieties that were resistant to disease, had manageable spiciness from pod to pod (so we could put them in our burritos without melting off our faces), and could be grown for mass consumption. His work paved the way for current cultivation techniques as well as the development and expansion of several chile varieties over the past decades. In 1975 NMSU horticulturalist Roy Nakayama released NuMex Big Jim, named for the Hatch farmer he worked with in development of the hybrid pepper. It is known for its meatiness and sturdy pod size and remains one of the state's most popular peppers.

Of course, the growing and harvest are just the beginning. After the peppers are roasted and peeled, cooks batter and stuff them for chiles rellenos and chop them to concoct sauces that find their way into enchiladas, burritos, pizzas, eggs, and just about everything else that's edible. Some of the pods remain in the fields to ripen to a brilliant red (or are hung on ristras to dry and brighten folks' homes) and are later boiled down into deep crimson sauces that warm us through the remainder of winter.

Despite the narrow growing and harvest season, both red and green chiles are available year-round thanks to canning and freezing. That means from January to December, you can ask for chile sauce that's red or green, or order both on the same plate, which we call Christmas.

While varieties grow throughout the state, Chile Central is the rural town of Hatch, just north of Las Cruces, where vast fields are nurtured by the Rio Grande. The peppers are harvested in the fall, and folks grab them by the bushel.

During my Las Cruces childhood, our family bypassed the grocery stores and markets in favor of farmers' stands set up right smackdab in the fields. On the ride home, our car would be filled with the aromas of farm dirt and green chile. That route was one of my earliest New Mexico food trails. I hope this guide will inspire you to revisit yours—or discover new ones.

2 Up and at 'Em
Breakfast Burritos and More

New Mexico breakfasts are often a dish of convenience. Scoop some eggs into a tortilla, add green chile and meat, bind it with cheese and potatoes, fold it, and hit the road. While the origins of the breakfast burrito are debatable (Tia Sophia's in Santa Fe claims to be the first to put it on a menu), what's not in question is that they're one of humanity's most perfect breakfast foods. And while the basic premise is to get the breakfast stuff into an edible wrapper, the nuances, especially here in New Mexico, run much deeper.

First and foremost, let's talk ingredients. The tortilla must be fresh and flavorful, preferably made on the spot. The eggs, cooked but not overcooked. The meat, spicy or smoky or both. Stuffed with hash browns or cubed potatoes? Some argue that they only take up room, but done just right, they can amp up the flavor profile and soak up the heat. The chile inside the burrito is key too, and some opt to add salsa in addition to red or green chile. And unless you'll be eating in the car (in which case order the handheld variety), consider the concept of "smothered," wherein the burrito is slathered in a pool of red or green chile sauce, or both (Christmas).

In short, the simple breakfast burrito is anything but, and you can eat one at any counter, food truck, or fancy establishment in the state and find something that each place does a bit differently. So don't get complacent: Make it your mission to try new options. And bring your appetite: The breakfast burritos at some restaurants in New Mexico protrude over the plate. So settle in and know that you're going to be there awhile.

The bacon biscuit sandwich from Manzanita Market in Taos is a hearty way to start the day.

Of course, breakfast burritos aren't the only morning game in town. Our beloved huevos rancheros, often made with blue corn tortillas and locally grown pintos, are what keep folks upright in the saddle. Prefer the sweet stuff? We have that too. When your stomach just can't start with a plate of red-hot chile, we have cinnamon rolls, doughnuts, and other delights featuring local pecans, piñons, and other regional flavors. And the pancakes? Blue corn, please.

Get an early start to check out this trail of breakfast options, and remember to pass the pecan syrup.

Taos

Manzanita Market

This well-curated, white-walled little eatery just off Taos Plaza looks as if Martha Stewart swept through, leaving an Instagrammable wake of beautiful New Mexican art and photogenic jars of preserved lemons and green beans. But this café offers more than a pretty face; its biscuits are so good that you might forget to post them on social media before you wolf them down. The bacon biscuit sandwich puts my favorite things together (bacon, eggs, cheese) under one buttery roof, then binds it all with a swipe of jalapeño honey butter. The biscuit itself, made with whole grains, is dense with butter but still manages some flake (so it's a little messy to eat with a fork). I wouldn't turn away anything else on the menu, including the half dozen or so varieties of house-made ice cream with revolving flavors that you won't find at Baskin-Robbins. Jennifer Hart is the hands-on owner here and also operates Taos's beloved Love Apple (theloveapple.net), a restaurant that specializes in organic, intimate dinners (cash or check only).

GOOD TO KNOW Closed Mondays. *103 N. Plaza. (575) 613–4088; manzanita market.net.*

Michael's Kitchen Restaurant and Bakery

Yes, Michael's offers premium examples of classic New Mexican breakfasts (breakfast enchiladas, burritos, huevos rancheros), but if I were heading up to Taos Ski Valley for a

Biscuits fill the breakfast bill at Manzanita Market in Taos.

Start your day with a doughnut or another house-baked goody at Michael's Kitchen Restaurant and Bakery in Taos.

day in the snow, I'd also want to grab one of those apple fritters from the bakery for an extra boost up the slopes. They're crispy, topped with a good distribution of apple chunks, and offer just the right amount of sweetness and moistness. The spongy cake doughnuts, topped with chocolate icing (which tastes like a rich ganache) and a few pecan sprinkles, comes in at a close second. Heck, maybe just get both. Also noteworthy: The cinnamon rolls are massive, as are the cream puffs, all of which are baked in Michael's basement pastry kitchen.

GOOD TO KNOW Open 7 a.m.–2 p.m. daily. *304-C N. Pueblo Road. (505) 758–4178; michaelskitchen.com.*

The breakfast burrito at Horseman's Haven Café fills the plate.

Santa Fe

El Chile Toreado

I do love the breakfast burritos here (made with two eggs, salsa, and, if you'd like, a meat combo of chorizo, bacon, and Polish sausage). The service is efficient, the burritos are perfectly proportioned to be easy to hold and not overly filling, and they contain just the right amount of heat to fire up the morning. But I also love the Toreado logo: two linked peppers that form the shape of a mustache. Formerly a small food cart near the Santa Fe Plaza and now just a slightly larger walk-up shack tucked away from the main tourist beat south of the Railyard district, this place doesn't have a dining room but is well-known among locals. Swing by, grab burritos and tacos (or even hot dogs, if you missed the breakfast hours), and chow down in the car or at your desk.

GOOD TO KNOW Breakfast is served until 10 a.m. Closes daily at 2:30 p.m. (2 p.m. on Saturdays). Closed Sundays.

opposite The breakfast burritos at Santa Fe's El Chile Toreado contain just the right amount of heat and meat.

807 Early Street. (505) 500–0033; elchiletoreado.com.

Horseman's Haven Café

Ranchers, state workers, road crews, and fancy business folks all gather at Horseman's at some time or another. The service is swift. "Café, hon?" the waitress asks in that recognizable *norteño* accent. "*Sí*. And keep it coming." The decor consists of simple wood-paneled walls and nondescript diner chairs and booths, but this is the place to go when you want a New Mexican comfort breakfast. Plenty of people will warn you that the green chile here is hot, and they won't be wrong. But don't be afraid—it's flavorful and worth the burn (in small quantities).

GOOD TO KNOW The folks won't look down on you here if you order your chile on the side, I promise. *4354 Cerrillos Road. (505) 471–5420.*

The Pantry

It's perfectly acceptable here to ponder the menu, ask your neighbors at the next table about the heat level on the chile, and order way more food than you should or can eat for your first meal of the day. This friendly, hometown spot, established on the busy Cerrillos corridor, has been here since 1948, and by the looks of the line stretching out the door, isn't going anywhere anytime soon. The smothered breakfast burrito is not for the lightweight appetite: This honker fills the plate and barely leaves room for the Pantry fries on the side (a must to soak up all that extra red and green chile). My go-to breakfast burrito has bacon, but the carne adovada option is always a good second (and makes for great leftovers if you can't finish it). The chile relleno omelet isn't too shabby, and if you're feeling the sweets, the blue corn pancakes or stuffed French toast will leave you full and happy.

GOOD TO KNOW The Pantry Dos ("two" in Spanish), opened in 2019, feeds folks on the South Side near Santa Fe Community College (closed Tuesdays). Yet another location, Pantry Rio, opened in fall 2020 near the plaza. *The Pantry: 1820 Cerrillos Road; (505) 986–0022. Pantry Dos: 20 White Feather; (505) 365–2859. Pantry Rio: 229 Galisteo Street; (505) 989–1919. pantry santafe.com; thepantrydos.com.*

La Plazuela, La Fonda

When I feel like playing tourist in my hometown, I go to La Fonda, my favorite piece of real estate in Santa Fe, on the corner of the plaza peering up at the Cathedral Basilica of St. Francis of Assisi. An original Harvey House designed by noted architect Mary Coulter, La Fonda and all its spaces were treated to a lovely facelift earlier this century, but the elements I love—the works painted by notable Southwest and Native artists that fill the lobby, the seating that allows you to watch the world stroll by, that feeling that I might have lived here in a past life—are always there. The hotel's signature La Plazuela café is almost always crowded, but on a weekday, before the morning rush, I grab a table and order one of my favorite

Santa Fe breakfasts: blue corn piñon pancakes with a side of bacon. The cakes are hearty but not heavy and come topped with a sprinkling of fresh berries and piñons, adding a little sweet, nutty flavor. The Chile Relleno con Huevos de Cualquier Estilo ("any style") shows the world that La Fonda's perfectly crispy and flavorful relleno is a good match for eggs and chile. After breakfast I meander out into the sunshine, gaze up at the church bathed in morning light, and take a quick walk around the plaza. All the dishes at La Plazuela, including the chile dishes, are at the top of the New Mexico cuisine game. Oddly, I occasionally crave Ethel's Chicken Salad Croissant, named for Ethel Ballen, who co-owned the hotel with husband, Sam, for fifty years. But no matter what I order, I'm in a place that's always in my heart.

GOOD TO KNOW La Fonda offers free docent-led tours of the hotel's art collection and architecture every Wednesday through Saturday. *100 E. San Francisco Street. (505) 982–5511; lafondasantafe.com.*

Albuquerque

TOP PICK

Duran Central Pharmacy

When the massive smothered breakfast burrito, measuring at least fourteen inches long, is first set before you, you might say, "Oh, my. How am I ever going to finish this thing?" But by the time you've wiped up the last puddle of chile with what remains of a mangled tortilla, you'll only be asking, "How am I going to fit through the door?" Yes, it's big. Yes, it's hot. Yes, you will probably eat the entire thing. Because it's so good. The allure here includes the massive, warm-your-heart, fresh-made flour tortillas, hand-rolled and cooked as the fixings for your burrito are grilled up. A tortilla hot off the grill is a magical thing—you can

The tortillas for massive breakfast burritos are made while you wait at Duran's in Albuquerque.

taste the love in each floury, charred-bubble bite. And if you don't get the burrito, I recommend ordering a tortilla on the side. It arrives in a pool of melted butter. I saw angels the last time I bit into one. As you look around at the curved counter and old-fashioned tables and tile, you'll find it no surprise that the magic here has been a few decades in the making. The pharmacy opened on this spot along Route 66 (after moving twice from nearby locations) in 1975. And while at its heart it is a pharmacy, the chile here might also cure what ails you. The blue corn enchilada plate will keep you young. As your tongue cools down, you can meander to the adjacent gift shop, which stocks a rich supply of New Mexico–made and –themed items, including hand-adorned dish towels, quirky jewelry, and soaps made with locally farmed lavender. And yes, you can also pick up a jar of Duran's red and green chile sauces. Angelic tortillas not included.

GOOD TO KNOW This little diner also serves wine and a selection of local beers, a good accompaniment to that hot chile. *1815 Central Avenue NW. (505) 247-4141; duransrx.com.*

Golden Pride BBQ, Chicken, and Ribs

Hardworking New Mexicans know that the best way to start a weekday (okay, a Monday) is with a fluffy, filling breakfast burrito from Golden Pride. The combo options are plentiful, but the basic—the "#1," which comes with scrambled egg, grated cheddar, hash browns, and green chile, all wrapped in one of GP's homemade tortillas—will cure Monday blues, even if you have to take it to go and eat it in the car or on the job. This regional chain is part of the famed Frontier restaurant group, where it's standard to find a big pot of warmed red chile to slather on to-go orders. Bonus? Golden Pride doesn't assign an arbitrary time to breakfast, so you can order one of these babies any time of day.

GOOD TO KNOW There are four convenient Duke City locations, and they all open at 6 a.m. on weekdays. *Central NE, (505) 293-3531; Central NW, (505) 836-1544; Lomas NE, (505) 242-2181; Juan Tabo NE, (505) 294-5767; goldenprideabq.com.*

Range Café

It's difficult to plug the Range into a category. It has the trappings of a diner, with bright New Mexico–quirky art covering the walls, food served on Fiestaware, and a nostalgic hominess that imbues all six of the Duke City–area locations. The Lizard Rodeo Lounge at the Bernalillo location pushes it toward the bar/beer hall category, and in the evening it could easily be mistaken for a New Mexico honky-tonk (or maybe a karaoke bar). The red and green chile served at this locally owned and operated chain makes it a must-stop if you're craving some good New Mexican fare. But out of all those elements, the breakfast menu seems to rise to the top. It's just really good comfort food—gloppy huevos rancheros served with blue corn tortillas, a

It's perfectly acceptable to have a sweet roll after a full breakfast at Albuquerque's Range Café.

New Mexico Benny made with green chile turkey sausage and chorizo-spiked hollandaise, papas con carne made with those addictive Range potatoes—that makes me lick my plate clean. The Range's cinnamon roll game is on target too, just in case you leave room (yes, in New Mexico, it's perfectly acceptable to have dessert with breakfast). You can walk it off by shopping at the Bernalillo location's Home at The Range gift shop, stocked with all the New Mexico–centric kitsch, art, and food items you could ask for (including a section that sells New Mexico–made spirits).

GOOD TO KNOW Multiple locations, each with its own distinct atmosphere and vibe. *Albuquerque: 10019 Coors Blvd. NW; (505) 835-5495. 4401 Wyoming Blvd. NE; (505) 293-2633. 1050 Rio Grande Blvd. NW; (505) 508-2640. 320 Central Avenue SE; (505) 243-1440. Bernalillo: 925 Camino del Pueblo; (505) 867-1700. Los Lunas: 740 Main Street NE; (505) 508-2144. rangecafe.com.*

Twisters

You might recognize Twisters from episodes of *Better Call Saul* and *Breaking*

Bad—it doubled as Los Pollos Hermanos, the notorious fast-food restaurant that played a key role in both series. But neither nefarious characters nor mysterious blue substances are required to enjoy this Albuquerque chain, which offers tasty burritos and other staples at reasonable prices. You'll find about a dozen breakfast burrito combinations that rearrange a variety of ingredients, including chile, bacon, ham, chorizo, carne adovada, beans, bell peppers, potatoes, and cheese, all of which you can get smothered or handheld and all in the $3.25–$8 range. The tacos, sandwiches, and Mexican classics plates are tempting, but who can resist the call of the breakfast burrito served all day?

GOOD TO KNOW The location that appeared on TV is at 4275 Isleta Boulevard SW and is often a stop on the Breaking Bad RV Tours (breakingbadrvtours.com), which take visitors to key Albuquerque filming sites in a retrofitted RV. *Eighteen locations in Albuquerque, Rio Rancho, Bernalillo, and Colorado; mytwisters.com.*

Twisters breakfast burritos are a local Albuquerque favorite.

Las Cruces

Santa Fe Grill, Pic Quik

Stay with me here: One of the best breakfast burritos in Las Cruces, and possibly in New Mexico, can be purchased at the same place you fill your gas tank. Yes, you'll find the Santa Fe Grill tucked inside ten Pic Quik locations, but don't be put off by the convenience store vibe. It's friendly, fast, and fresh, and the burritos are made to eat on the road. Bacon, beans, veggies, turkey, chorizo, and other items are there for the choosing, and you can watch as the cook works the small grill with the skill and artistry of a hibachi chef, spinning the eggs, potatoes, green chile, and cheese into a grill-warmed tortilla. The menu is extensive, and while I can't bear to stray from the beloved burrito, others swear that the Ultimate Breakfast Sandwich, made with egg, provolone, and meat of your choice, is equally transcendent. The non–breakfast burritos are legendary too (the Kid Dynamite made with a chile relleno and chorizo is a good call) and will fill up all the tanks.

GOOD TO KNOW Because these burritos are made to order, you'll probably experience a wait during peak breakfast hours. *Multiple locations throughout Las Cruces; sfgrillnm.com.*

Silver City

Diane's Restaurant

Silver City is an arts town, but because of its relative isolation in New Mexico—it's tucked near the 3.3 million–acre Gila National Forest and is more than one hundred miles from Las Cruces via mountain roads—creating a foodie scene to accompany its creative side is a challenge. Thankfully, Diane Barrett came to town more than

two decades ago and opened a small bakery. She expanded in 1997 with the opening of her restaurant and lounge, which fits the foodie bill pretty well. Her lunch and dinner offerings are well crafted and made with expert chef hands, but my favorite so far is breakfast, where her Hatch Benedict provides a nice break from standard burrito or diner fare. Each layer is carefully considered, starting with a porous but crispy chile cheddar toast that's happy to soak up the yolk of a deftly poached egg. The hollandaise is buttery and smooth and mixes sublimely with the ham, green chile, and zing of jalapeño. On top is a garlicy salsa that gives it all a satisfying tomato twang. (See the sweets chapter for more about Diane's baked goods.)

GOOD TO KNOW The adjacent Diane's Parlor offers grown-up beverages and an upscale pub menu. *510 N. Bullard Street. (575) 538–8722; dianesrestaurant.com.*

Carlsbad

PJ & B Rio Café

For kids who grew up on the drier eastern side of New Mexico and the western edge of Texas, a trip to Carlsbad was always a treat. Sure, there's Carlsbad Caverns National Park, but even more captivating were the cooling waters of the Pecos River, winding its way through the hardscrabble desert. On a bright summer day, there was no greater relief. These days, the river offers boating, a water park, and the Pecos River Village Recreational Center, which features a river walk and, yes, places to grab a bite. The PJ & B is tucked into one of the renovated pink buildings overlooking the Pecos and offers a lineup of breakfast burritos that will feed any river adventure. The menu offers more than forty hearty burrito options (for breakfast and lunch), with ingredients ranging from steak with barbecue sauce to brisket and jalapeño. A popular morning option is the Breakfast Lover, which is packed with ham, sausage, bacon, potato, egg, cheese, and pico de gallo—it's a workout just to lift it.

GOOD TO KNOW Grab your burritos to go and then sit on the banks of the Pecos River, which is especially inviting during the summer months. *711 Muscatel Avenue. (575) 689-7305.*

While You're Here: Carlsbad

This is oil and gas country, so expect to see a town filled with roughnecks and big trucks. But Carlsbad has a softer side too, with a focus on nature and the great outdoors. Check out these highlights:

CARLSBAD CAVERNS NATIONAL PARK If you think all caves look alike, then you haven't been to Carlsbad Caverns. After you descend 750 feet into the earth, you will wind through such rooms as the Bat Cave, Mystery Room, and Hall of Giants. Each room is artistically lit to spotlight the stalactites, stalagmites, draperies, cave pearls, and other beautiful formations. Visitors can also take a lantern tour to see the caves in their more natural state, just as early explorers did. Or cast aside your claustrophobia for a ranger-led tour of Slaughter Canyon Cave, which takes visitors through narrow passageways lit only by lanterns. Early birds can grab breakfast burritos and wait for dawn, when clouds of Mexican free-tailed bats make their return to the caves after a nightly feast on the bugs of Carlsbad, one of nature's most dramatic and jaw-dropping shows. *nps.gov/cave/index.htm.*

LIVING DESERT ZOO AND GARDENS STATE PARK Howl with Mexican wolves, wave to the elks, marvel at the grace of mountain lions, enjoy the antics of a black bear and more than forty other species of desert birds, mammals, and reptiles at this scenic, meandering park. The flora is worth the hike too, and visitors can pause for picnics at lookouts that offer striking views of the Chihuahuan Desert surrounding Carlsbad. *emnrd.state.nm.us.*

SITTING BULL FALLS RECREATION AREA You wouldn't necessarily know it at first glance, but this slice of New Mexico holds some of the state's most dramatic scenery. Case in point: Sitting Bull Falls, a surprisingly lush park located forty-three miles southwest of Carlsbad, hiding natural pools and waterfalls. Hiking trails and picnicking abound, and a dip in the water is the best antidote to the desert heat of the Guadalupe Mountains. *fs.usda.gov.*

A NOTE ABOUT HOTELS Oil is a major economic driver in New Mexico, and the industry is going strong in this part of the state. Visitors might experience hotel-rate sticker shock since companies need to house large numbers of workers, putting hotel rooms at a premium. You'll find a few fun options that cater to visitors, including the beautifully renovated and historic Trinity Hotel and Restaurant (which also houses a resident ghost, naturally). The Fiddler's Inn Bed and Breakfast offers well-appointed rooms that are cozy and homey, furnished with antiques and designer touches. *thetrinityhotel.com; fiddlersinnbb.com.*

3 What'll Ya Have, Honey?
Diners and Dives

How do you define a diner? For some, it's the classic greasy spoon, a place with plastic-covered menus, booths that could use a good scrubbing, and a bacon-and-eggs plate you can count on. For others, a diner should have an element of nostalgia, with black-and-white-tiled floors and thick milkshakes made with real ice cream and delivered by servers in uniforms. There are also those places that aren't necessarily nostalgic but won't mind if your toddler drops crackers on the floor or that just serve really good food in a comfortable setting. All those (and more) are what this chapter is about.

My parents met and had their first date at Hiebert's Fine Foods, a now-defunct but once glorious Formica-countered diner in Las Cruces that specialized in steak fingers. And I remember many times trekking with my family as a kid to Vip's Big Boy Restaurant, where I'd try to wrap my arms around the belly of the fiberglass statue of the boy mascot out front and reveled in the fact that I could have both hot chocolate and pancakes for dinner.

If you're taking a foodie road trip in New Mexico, especially along the old Route 66 (roughly Interstate 40), you're likely to encounter one of those nostalgic eateries along the Mother Road, which stretches 2,448 miles from Chicago to Santa Monica. It's because of this legendary road that the diner trend was born and continues to live on in America.

In New Mexico, the diner scene runs from kitschy to trendy, from blue plate specials to red and green combos. The following restaurants are listed here because they offer something special, whether it's friendly folks, good eats, or a dose of nostalgia (or all three!), that make them worth going the extra mile.

Santa Fe

Harry's Roadhouse

If you want to hang with the locals, this is the place to do it. But be forewarned: This place gets packed, especially during peak dining times. You'll be able to tell by all the cars filling the dirt parking lot, but don't be discouraged. The eclectic menu, friendly service, and relaxed, artsy atmosphere make this a good roadside stop. I've yet to have a disappointing meal here. I favor the moist and tangy lemon ricotta pancakes at breakfast, the blue corn–turkey enchiladas at lunch, and the eggplant parmesan pizza for dinner. The pie case (pecan is my go-to) displaying a range of house-made treats is a persistent temptation. And if you have to wait for a table? You can order a margarita to sip while you wait. (Read more in the margaritas chapter.)

GOOD TO KNOW Local artists design the T-shirts offered for sale here, and they're cool. *96B Old Las Vegas Highway. (505) 989–4629; harrysroadhousesantafe .com.*

Plaza Café

A number of our favorite northern New Mexican restaurants were established by Greek families who immigrated here, and the Plaza Café is no exception. During a time when the roads around Santa Fe were made of dirt (okay, maybe not that much has changed) and New Mexico was yet to become the forty-seventh state in 1912, the Ipiotis brothers opened the Star Restaurant on the plaza in 1905. It then passed through a few other capable Greek hands, along the way becoming the Plaza Café, and was purchased in the 1940s by Dan Razatos, whose family still runs the venerable diner. The result is a modern-day menu that reflects diner sensibilities—hearty breakfasts, tantalizing baked goods, friendly service—with New Mexican– and Greek-influenced dishes that range from green chile meat loaf to gyros. No matter which nationality you favor, the café is a good place to fuel up during a jaunt downtown, and you can always find some old-fashioned hospitality.

GOOD TO KNOW Avoid the tourist crush by checking out the Plaza Café Southside location at 3466 Zafarano Drive (plazacafe south.com). *54 Lincoln Avenue. (505) 982–1664; plazacafesantafe.com.*

Las Vegas

Charlie's Spic and Span

In the mid-1800s, Las Vegas was the biggest city in what would become New Mexico in a few decades. It was an entry point for the Old Santa Fe Trail, a major travel and trade route, and a stop along the Atchison, Topeka, and Santa Fe Railway. It was home to a cluster of Teddy Roosevelt's Rough Riders; saw its share of gunslingers, such as Doc Holliday and Billy the Kid; and was home to a few Harvey Houses, a group of well-appointed and high-quality hotels and restaurants that became a beacon for western travelers. Las Vegas has lost a bit of its big-city

luster over the years, but thanks to an active historic preservation community and a desire to bring its beautiful buildings back to life, it's become a hidden gem of a town (with nearly one thousand buildings on the National Register of Historic Places). It is packed with surprises—including Charlie's. During my first visit there, after I finished breakfast, the waitress came by, filled my coffee cup, and innocently said, "You ready for a cinnamon bun?"

"Oh, no, I couldn't. Wait. What?"

I guess it's standard for some folks to top off with one of the restaurant's homemade treats, even if they've just tanked up on the breakfast skillet of green chile, crispy cubed potatoes, and eggs. The fluffy flour tortillas are made in-house too, and you can watch them roll off the tortilla machine as you ponder whether you're finishing your meal with a two-story cream puff or an apple fritter.

GOOD TO KNOW Jars of Charlie's red and green sauces can be purchased at the restaurant or on the restaurant's website. *715 Douglas Avenue. (505) 426–1921; charliesbakeryandcafe.com.*

Gallup

Jerry's Café

I have a friend who drives a "mapping unit" truck to create maps that don't require a cell tower but rather an innate ability to fold an oversize piece of paper in a very specific way. That means he knows every inch of New Mexico's back roads as well as the best place to shop for a sturdy but stylish cowboy hat and where to get a good meal in the middle of nowhere. A favorite place in his vast mapping territory is Jerry's, where he knows he can get his fix of hot chile and friendly people, many of whom love to chat him up about the mapping unit. This place is no-frills, and the wood paneling might give you a flashback to your grandma's dining room. But the food is fresh and filling and the humans welcoming, fulfilling the main requirements of a good rural diner. Jerry's Chile Relleno con Huevos gets my vote, but the burgers and stuffed sopaipillas get high marks too. And if you get lost out here? Just watch for the mapping unit.

GOOD TO KNOW Closed Sundays. Vendors often come in selling Native American jewelry. *406 W. Coal Avenue. (505) 722–6775.*

Albuquerque

66 Diner

Some of us recall a time when you pulled into a service station and got actual service: fluid check, window cleaning, an attendant in a uniform and cap who pumped your gas. The stations were architectural beauties bathed in neon, and the pumps were themselves works of art. Well, those days are long gone, but thanks to the nostalgia of Route 66, some places held on to the aesthetic—and took it up a notch. In 1987 this building was converted from a shapely Phillips 66 service station to a diner that today celebrates its Route 66 roots. Those black-and-white checkerboard tiles, brushed aluminum backsplashes, servers in uniforms, and walls of road signs inside and out create a lively atmosphere that will make you want to go to a sock hop in your jalopy—or at least have a burger and a shake. Speaking of which, the menu strikes a comfort food chord of yore, with chicken and dumplings, burgers smothered in queso or green chile stew (a humble concoction of pork and potato chunks cooked with green chiles, onion, and garlic), housemade pies, and more. The malts and milkshakes are magnificent, with twenty flavors ranging from caramel apple to chocolate-covered strawberry.

GOOD TO KNOW You'll receive a free shake if you sign up for the 66 Diner

Cruiser Club (and a free meal on your birthday). Breakfast served only from 8 a.m. to noon on Saturdays and Sundays. *1405 Central Avenue NE. (505) 247–1421; 66diner.com.*

TOP PICK

Frontier Restaurant

University of New Mexico students have been getting big plates of food for a reasonable price here since this famed eatery opened in 1971. I like to enjoy my breakfast burrito under the watchful eye of the life-size John Wayne cardboard cutout, and neither ever disappoints. The restaurant makes its own fluffy tortillas, and the red salsa is kept warm in big heated pots. I'm pretty sure the home-cooked vibe is what attracts the students and other regulars. Posole (a red chile–based stew with pork or chicken and hominy), green chile stew, nachos, and the beef and bean burrito all make us feel a little less homesick. And with the large portions, it's easy to overlook the sweet rolls—but don't even try to resist them. They come slightly warmed, and the buttery, gooey frosting oozes through the twists of dough, covering it all in a sugary veneer. Take it with you if you must, but the college student rule is gospel: Don't leave without ordering one.

GOOD TO KNOW Open daily 5 a.m.–10 p.m., with all menu items served around the clock. *2400 Central Avenue SE. (505) 266–0550; frontierrestaurant.com.*

Range Café

Owners Tom Fenton and Matt DiGregory took the old diner concept and raised the bar with their Range Cafés, a regional mini-chain of restaurants offering home-cooked comfort food with a flavorful twist. The food runs the New Mexican and American gambit—huevos rancheros, biscuits and gravy, green chile cheeseburgers, and chicken mole enchiladas—all of it prepared

The Range Café offers New Mexico comfort foods, including huevos rancheros and crispy home fries.

fresh and at a level above standard diner fare. The decor is best described as rustic New Mexican, with homegrown art, playful 3D murals, and brightly painted, chunky Mexican-style furniture. Each of the six locations has its own touches and is worth a visit. The former Standard Diner, part of the Range's restaurant group, was converted to Range Café Central in fall 2020, and plans called for an upgraded adult beverage menu

Route 66 for Kicks

We take this stuff for granted: wide-open views, desert scrub–covered vistas, ghost towns with photogenically worn service stations, and lonely stretches of highway where the pronghorns outnumber the people. While we often look at these long-distance drives on lonely highways as something to be endured, visitors from other countries and continents find them fascinating. That's one reason the mystique of America's famed Mother Road, Route 66, endures, calling out to those in search of neon signs and rustic motor lodges. New Mexico's portion stretches 399 miles across the state's middle (it was originally 507 miles but was rerouted south of Santa Fe in 1937), and when the interstate highway system came along and the route was decommissioned, it left behind the bones of another America. One way to honor the route is to pull off, explore, and have a milkshake or a chicken-fried steak at one of the remaining restaurants, many of them an homage to Route 66's ghosts. Let's take a quick trip across the New Mexico portion, from east to west.

TUCUMCARI The bright neon sign of the Blue Swallow Motel is like a beacon to weary travelers as they enter New Mexico from Texas. The rooms manage to be both basic and adorable, revamped with period furnishings and other touches. Next-door is Tee Pee Curios, where fans can stock up on Route 66 souvenirs in the confines of a concrete teepee. Swing by the New Mexico Route 66 Museum, which is stocked with photos, posters, and other relics of the route's heyday.

SANTA ROSA Gearheads should gun it for the Route 66 Auto Museum, where longtime resident James "Bozo" Cordova has been restoring old cars for more than forty years. More than thirty cars are on display here, capturing some cool, chromed, hot-rodding history.

TIJERAS On a little jog of Route 66 about twenty miles east of Albuquerque is the Route 66 Musical Highway. If you drive exactly at the 45 mph speed

and another Lizard Rodeo Lounge installation. Don't worry; the bacon-wrapped meat loaf sandwich is still on the menu. (Read more in the breakfast chapter.)

GOOD TO KNOW The Home at The Range gift shop at the Bernalillo location offers wine and spirits tastings as well as book and poetry readings by local authors. (The *At Home with the Range Café* cookbook is for sale here too.) *Albuquerque: 10019 Coors Blvd. NW; (505) 835–5495. 4401 Wyoming Blvd. NE; (505) 293–2633. 1050 Rio Grande Blvd. NW; (505) 508–2640. 320 Central Avenue SE; (505) 243-1440. Bernalillo:*

925 Camino del Pueblo; (505) 867–1700. Los Lunas: 740 Main Street NE; (505) 508–2144. rangecafe.com.

Tucumcari

Kix on 66

Here's the traditional diner you've been looking for. Patrons can belly up to a counter that peeks into the kitchen, plus the place offers nostalgic Route 66 decor to go with its perfectly crispy hash browns. Diners rave about all the dishes here,

limit, your tires will hum the tune of "America the Beautiful." The ridges in the road are getting a little worn, so the tune isn't as clear (the musical stretch was built back in 2014), but it's still a piece of the old road that's worth taking.

ALBUQUERQUE This is Route 66 Central, which is fitting, since Route 66 ran right through the center of town on a street that is now called Central Avenue. Before a 1937 realignment, the route ran through Santa Fe. Post-alignment, it slices eighteen miles through the heart of Albuquerque, where several hotels, attractions, and eateries that popped up during the Route 66 heyday remain. Highlights include the art deco KiMo Theater (opened in 1927 and still functioning as a performance space) and El Vado Motel, which was built in 1937 and revamped in 2018 with hipster charm and modern comforts such as a craft brewery and shops stocked with locally made (and some Route 66–centric) products.

GALLUP Route 66 would not be what it is today without the contributions and presence of indigenous people. Gallup sits at the edge of the more than 27,000-square-mile Navajo Nation, which overlaps with three states. Nearby also are the Zuni and Hopi Pueblos. This area is rich with ways to explore and appreciate those cultures through artwork, traditional dance performances, and other contributions. Learn more by exploring Gallup's trading posts along Route 66. On Saturdays, visit the Gallup Ninth Street Flea Market, one of the nation's biggest Native American markets. Meander through Hotel El Rancho, where celebrities often stayed while filming westerns nearby. The lobby is reminiscent of the Old West, filled with cowboy sculptures, Navajo rugs, taxidermy, and wagon-wheel furniture.

including the smothered burrito and the pancakes (called "pankix" here). The waffle fries that come with the sandwiches are also a standout. In fact, this place has a special affinity for potatoes, given that there's a dish on the menu called the Tucumcari Mountain of Taters, which comes with red or green chile, eggs, and a choice of other toppings.

GOOD TO KNOW Open 6 a.m.–2 p.m. *1102 E. Route 66. (575) 461–1966.*

Hatch

The Pepper Pot

The sleepy little farming town of Hatch is not so sleepy during chile harvest season, usually between late July and September. It's an exciting time for pepper fans, who clean out freezers and pantries in preparation for this annual harvest. But the best part is experiencing the peppers as they are pulled from the field and plopped right onto your plate. To that end, the chiles rellenos are a top choice at this darling little eatery. They're crisp, cheesy, and can be slathered in your chile of choice (green for me on this one). And while this place doesn't have the traditional diner atmosphere, its *papel picados* (decorative cut tissue paper), red-tiled floors, and general showiness place it in a special "Mexican diner" category.

GOOD TO KNOW Open daily 7 a.m.– 3 p.m. *250 W. Hall Street. (575) 267–3822.*

Las Cruces

Dick's Café

As hungry journalism students attending New Mexico State University, many of us favored this old-school Las Cruces haunt, which opened in 1959. (That was significantly before I started going there, for the record.) It still bears the classic 1950s decor, with checkered floors and table tops that advertise local businesses, and like many of its kind in the state, it does double duty by serving both diner food and New Mexican cuisine. As college students, we went here mostly for the green chile cheeseburgers (and the hand-cut fries are the bomb), but since my palate is so much more refined these days, I also yearn for a dose of the restaurant's green chile. And the enchilada plate with an egg on top is food for the soul.

GOOD TO KNOW The restaurant also serves beer and wine. Fans also can buy Dick's salsa and green sauce online. *2305 S. Valley Drive. (575) 524–1360; dicks-cafe.com.*

Roswell

Big D's Downtown Dive

It says "dive" right in the name of the place, and while this cool little eatery isn't fancy, it easily transcends the diner malaise, both in looks and cuisine. Walk toward the wall of New Mexico license plates to place your order, which, if you're smart, will include the green chile cheesesteak. The burger menu is extensive and popular—the breakfast burger will take care of those in your party who aren't ready to give up their bacon-and-egg dreams just because it's one o'clock in the afternoon. (And to further the cause, the bacon is smoked with pecan wood.) Fried tater fans can dive into the Monster Fries, a mound of the fried guys topped with a creamy house-made sauce, green chile, and some of that aforementioned pecan-smoked bacon.

GOOD TO KNOW Cheesesteaks are two for $12 on Wednesdays. First responders and veterans receive a 15 percent discount. *505 N. Main Street. (575) 627–0776.*

4 Two Worlds Collide
The Green Chile Cheeseburger

You can find cheeseburgers in every state in the union, but not like the ones in New Mexico. Here, the simple combo of meat, cheese, and bun—plus our beloved green chile—has spawned social media worship and live smackdowns lending serious street cred to those with the right skills. Their creations range from simple one-handers to towers that can barely be squished down to fit into even the most ambitious chomp.

This trail, even with a few vegetarian options added in, is best made in short jaunts—or at least while sporting an elastic waistband. These burgers are serious affairs.

How has the simple New Mexico–spun burger evolved into such an art form, you ask? The ingredients are basic, but the ways in which they're prepared vary widely. While sometimes you just need the simple fast-food remedy (New Mexico's top GCCB chain Blake's Lotaburger will scratch that itch), elements of these burgers can also transcend the norm and put you on the path to enlightenment.

Let's start with the meat. You can go smash, open flame, spiced, thick, sirloin, bison (often New Mexico born and bred), bacon, and black bean. The buns? Think ciabatta, brioche, or sesame. Do you want your chile chopped or deep-fried? With garnish or a cappella? How about a special sauce? Want house-made chips, potato wedges, or onion rings on the side? And would you like a dip with those?

Like the burgers themselves, the spots serving them range from low-key to lavish and will infuse variety into craving-inspired road trips that might take you halfway across the state. So hang on and let this protein-packed chapter serve as your trusted burger backseat driver.

New Mexico's green chile cheeseburger is the perfect combo of meat, cheese, and chile.

Farmington

3 Rivers Brewery Block

John Silva loves to feed people good food. He loves hospitality and ensuring that people have a good time. And it shows. Silva has been slowly buying up the historic buildings in downtown Farmington adjacent to his first restaurant and brewery, on the corner of Main Street and Orchard Avenue, and has transformed them into what he calls the 3 Rivers Brewery Block. There's now also a pizzeria and a beautifully designed "brewstillery" lounge (read more in the wine and spirits chapter). The beer, the rustic decor (most of it collected or built by Silva), and the overall vibe prompt an "Are you sure we're still in Farmington?" feel, and the food is far from small town. For starters, the green chile cheeseburger pairs perfectly with 3 Rivers' Merica American pale ale. The *telera* buns (rolls that are staples at Mexican bakeries, often used for tortas) are imported from La Brea Bakery in SoCal, but the rest is pure New Mexico. "I refuse to cut open a bag," Silva says. A whiff of Hatch-grown, extra-hot chile fills the nose before you even take a bite, and after the bite, you can feel the burn in your chest (hence the need for the appropriate ale). "Do you order ice cream and say it's too cold?" says Silva. From many of the seats in the front part of the restaurant, you can watch as the kitchen applies the perfect char to the patties, which are made fresh from brisket ground in-house, cooked medium rare, and spiced only with salt and pepper—that's "all a burger needs if it's good," Silva notes. Atmosphere? The restaurant has that too. The walls are covered with antiques Silva has gathered around town, as well as a few relics he found when he bought the building, a former drugstore.

GOOD TO KNOW The 3 Rivers Game and Tap Room next door is a fun hangout for families, with pool tables, foosball, and arcade video games. *101 E. Main Street. (505) 324–2187; threeriversbrewery.com.*

AshKii's Navajo Grill

Forget the two-hander burger; this is easily made for three hands. The Big Boy Burger comes with three patties, is topped with lettuce and tomato, and is served atop a glistening half circle of one of humankind's tastiest inventions: fry bread. On top of the heap is a freshly roasted green chile pod. You have to peel the chile yourself, but hey, at least you know it's fresh. My first clue that this would be a messy affair was that each table is adorned with a roll—that's right, a roll—of paper towels. The food is worth the mess. The addition of fry bread takes the Navajo version of the green chile cheeseburger to new and creative heights. The fry bread mingles well with the burger patties and to me represents cultures coming together, all in the name of a delicious meal. Diners can also opt for the more

AshKii's Navajo Grill in Farmington gives the traditional green chile cheeseburger a fry bread flourish.

traditional mutton. Sheep are an important part of the Navajo culture, raised for both meat and wool.

GOOD TO KNOW The fry bread here is great by itself. *123 W. Broadway. (505) 326-3804.*

Abiquiú

Bodes General Store

Surprise: Gas station grill serves great food! Bodes is a general store and gas station that has become a hot roadside spot in Abiquiú, a quiet, artsy town near the hill where artist Georgia O'Keeffe really plunged into those New Mexico landscapes. Marked by a giant pink flamingo in the parking lot, the market has a wicked kitchen that whomps up one of northern New Mexico's best GCCBs. The meaty, flavorful patty is juicy, the chile has kick, and the sesame seed bun gives it a nostalgic home-cooked feel. The only complaint is that the oversize hunk of green leaf lettuce gets in the way of the meat–cheese–chile umami, but it's easy to trim it down or, better yet, peel it off. The fries are cut fresh and are delish, but I lean toward the fresh tots, which are deep-fried to provide the perfect grease-crisped potato delivery system. Feeling the need to mix it up? The Green Chile Philly is a good break from the norm, with salty sliced beef forming a brilliant partnership with the heat of the chile.

Bodes General Store serves a juicy green chile cheeseburger in its Abiquiú café.

Then walk it off by checking out the store's New Mexico–themed merchandise, such as locally made artwork, regional snacks, and beers.

GOOD TO KNOW You'll find New Mexico gifts here, as well as provisions for fishing and camping trips. *21196 U.S. 84. (505) 685-4422; bodes.com.*

Santa Fe

Cowgirl Santa Fe

Anyone who forgets that Santa Fe is a western town can reclaim that swagger by ducking into Cowgirl. A rustic vibe, with servers in cowboy hats and boots, and plenty of meaty menu options (including solid entries in the barbecue category) evoke a gussied-up version of the classic cowboy hangout. Even if you haven't been punching cows on the trail or herding horses into corrals, you're eligible to enjoy the restaurant's signature Mother of All Green Chile Cheeseburgers. At its base is a patty blended with beef and buffalo that supports a thick slice of apple-wood-smoked bacon. The use of brie rather than cheddar elevates it to gourmet status, and while I think a standard cheddar would fit the bill, I appreciate the fact that this burger likes to set itself apart with a bit of fussiness. The buttery cheddar–green chile roll holds it together, even when the burger juice runs down the palm of your hand. On the side are crispy truffle waffle fries, which I scarfed down even though the burger had clearly filled me up. On select evenings, live musicians might inspire you to work off the burger by taking a spin on the little dance floor in front of the even tinier stage next to the bar. In another room is a spacious pool hall, another way to kill a few calories in western ambience.

GOOD TO KNOW This place gets hopping on weekends, especially during the summer, so plan on waiting for a table during peak times. *319 S. Guadalupe Street. (505) 982–2565; cowgirlsantafe.com.*

Del Charro

Here's my question, New Mexico: Why aren't we squishing red chile into and on top of our patties more often? Is it because the green chile peeps have better marketing? I've eaten more green chile cheeseburgers than I can count, and I sure could go for a red chile option. Why isn't this a thing? At Del Charro, Santa Fe's answer to a locals' sports bar, you have to time this one just right; the red chile burger is not on the regular menu but is the daily special on weekends. The patty has red chile sauce worked into the beef, with a generous dose of house-made red sauce between the patty and the bun. The burger comes with tomato, lettuce, and onion but, curiously, no cheese. For whatever reason, this concoction works and will sweep the nation if the red lovers ever get their act together and start battling Camp Green. The chips are made in-house too, and if you should

The green chile cheeseburger at El Farol in Santa Fe is a bacon lover's delight.

accidentally drip a bit of red chile on them, you'll enjoy that happy accident.

GOOD TO KNOW Keep an eye on the daily specials menu, which features delicious surprises. *101 W. Alameda Street. (505) 954–0320; delcharro.com.*

El Farol

"If we're going to put something like a cheeseburger on the menu, it's going to be great," says Richard Freedman, who co-owns the restaurant with general manager Freda Scott. Mission accomplished. With a custom-blended, eight-ounce patty made with ground brisket and infused with flavorful bone marrow, and then topped with bacon selected via rigorous in-house taste-testing, El Farol has found its queen, the Hamburguesa Santa Fe. It's topped with a butter lettuce leaf, a layer of cheddar draped over chopped green chile, bread and butter pickles, and a green chile–specked brioche bun that is croissant-like in its ability to soak up the juice. The artsy Canyon Road vibe of this historic building only adds to the dining experience, which can be made even greater with the addition of the house margarita. (Read more in the margaritas chapter.)

GOOD TO KNOW The live music and flamenco make for a lively evening out, but if

above Try the smoky, rich red chile burger at Del Charro in Santa Fe.

opposite Cowgirl Santa Fe's Mother of All Green Chile Cheeseburgers blends a beef and buffalo patty with bacon and brie.

Santa Fe locals favor the flavorful green chile cheeseburger and crispy ribbon fries at the Original Realburger.

friendly folks behind the counter who take my order. The dining room resembles your aunt's kitchen, with pithy sayings posted about and vinyl tablecloths. There's a mural depicting a map, our high desert mountains with aspens, and roadrunners—all components that point to state pride. And the green chile cheeseburgers? They taste like homemade backyard burgers. The patties are hand formed and well crisped at the edges. They come naked so that you can belly up to the condiment station, where you load up with everything from shredded iceberg and raw onions to jalapeños and pico de gallo. The fresh-cut fries are great, but the ribbon fries are even greater. I try to share but inevitably end up swatting those hands that reach for my ribbons.

GOOD TO KNOW Closed Sundays. *2641–1/2 Cerrillos Road. (505) 474-7325.*

you want to keep it a little more low-key, hit up El Farol at happy hour from 3 to 5 p.m. *808 Canyon Road. (505) 983–9912; elfarol santafe.com.*

The Original Realburger

There's the postcard Santa Fe and then there's the locals' version. The latter is the Santa Fe that cruises Cerrillos Road, the town's main commerce artery, hits the Santa Fe Place Mall on the regular, or rolls through Sonic for two-for-one cherry limeades during the fast-food chain's famed happy hour (2–4 p.m. daily). This part of Santa Fe appears to be all chains and no substance, but visitors are often surprised to find several culinary gems among the sea of fast-food joints and '70s-style state office buildings. These are the places we locals have declared our own, and Realburger is one such outpost. I feel like I know the

Santa Fe Bite has perfected its juicy, ten-ounce honker, which draws locals and tourists alike.

Santa Fe Bite

Believe it or not, New Mexico's green chile cheeseburger craze is a relatively recent invention (or at least the marketing of it is). I'm a homegrown New Mexican, but Santa Fe Bite gave me my formal introduction to Santa Fe's contemporary version of this dish a few years ago, and it lit a fire in my belly to seek out more of these wonders throughout the state. Owners John and Bonnie Eckre took over in 2013, and the restaurant has moved around a bit since it first opened as Bobcat Bite more than six decades ago out on Old Las Vegas Highway, but the burger has stood the test of time. A thick ten-ounce patty (they offer a six ounce, by why would you?) made from local beef takes the lead on flavor. Its perfect char mushes beautifully with a hearty, cornmeal-crusted brioche bun from Fano Bakery in Albuquerque. A layer of melted white cheese holds a generous scoop of diced green chile (Hatch, natch) in place. All you have to do is fit that into your mouth. A side of house-made chips rounds out the plate, making it a challenge to squeeze in a slice of house-made pie or cookies for dessert.

GOOD TO KNOW The food is a little pricier than you might expect for a family diner—a GCCB is about $13—but it's worth it. And Duke City residents now have their own location. *Santa Fe: 1616 St. Michael's Drive; (505) 428–0328. Albuquerque: 3407 Central Avenue NE; (505) 369–1621. santafe bite.com.*

Shake Foundation

Is there any better pairing than a juicy cheeseburger and a chocolate shake? Maybe, if you add green chile to that burger. Shake Foundation does it right, using a specially blended sirloin and brisket patty. And the creamy shake is almost a requirement to put out the green chile burn. Just don't leave the hand-cut

The shoestring fries are as big a draw as the burgers at Santa Fe's Shake Foundation.

shoestring fries out of the equation; they're some of the best in the state (and might even rate higher for me than the burger). Enjoy it all on the outdoor picnic benches tucked under tall shade trees, one of the prettier outdoor dining spots that's not on the plaza.

GOOD TO KNOW Hours change seasonally, so call ahead. *631 Cerrillos Road. (505) 988–8992.*

Las Vegas

TOP PICK

Bar Castaneda

This green chile cheeseburger is love at first bite. Let's start by talking about chef Sean Sinclair's buns, shall we? He's cooked up a house-made Japanese milk bun, with just a touch of sweetness but firm enough to hold the meat, which is smashed rather than

While You're Here: Santa Fe

Santa Fe's vast and varied attractions make it difficult to craft a short list, but this three-day itinerary should give you an idea of how to pack in activities between all those great meals and margaritas.

DAY ONE Mornings on Museum Hill are a good start, given the choice of attractions: the Wheelwright Museum of the American Indian, the Museum of Indian Arts and Culture, the Museum of Spanish Colonial Art, the Museum of International Folk Art, and the Santa Fe Botanical Garden. They're all great, but if you have limited time, hit MoIFA, fuel up on the house-made portobello mushroom taquitos at Weldon's Museum Hill Café, and stroll through the sculptures and desert plant displays at the botanical garden. Then have a cup of tea or a mimosa at the Teahouse on famed Canyon Road before meandering along the narrow, half-mile road lined with more than one hundred art galleries, boutiques, and cafés.

DAY TWO Start early to beat the lines that form at Meow Wolf (tip: buy your tickets online and avoid the wait), a bizarre art collective inside a former bowling alley that is guarded in the parking lot by a giant spider and a robot. It's weird, but you'll love it. You can follow a narrative about a family that gets sucked into a place between time and space or you can just wander and discover the cool interactive art pieces. The concert venue here attracts an indie lineup of musicians and other performers. After you've found your way out of the gift shop, be sure to sit in Float Café and Bar and grab a Meowgarita topped with a cotton candy cloud.

DAY THREE Yes, more museums are on the agenda today. The New Mexico History Museum provides a solid overview of our great state and spits you out near the recently renovated Palace of the Governors, outside of which local Native American artists set up blankets and sell their jewelry, pottery, and other art. Don't leave without visiting the Georgia O'Keeffe Museum, which shows that she was much more than giant flower and cow skull artist. If you're in town between June and August, don't let me hear you whine, "I don't like opera." You'll miss world-class performances in front of a dramatic high-desert backdrop at Santa Fe Opera. Yes, it's opera, but it's arguably one of the most beautiful places to experience it. Imagine a stormy desert night, lightning filling the skies, sopranos hitting high notes, beautiful costumes, and eye-popping sets. Tailgating is elevated here—you can order special picnics forty-eight hours in advance on the opera website.

If you truly can't stomach Italian arias, you can still opt for a backstage tour, offered at 9 a.m. Monday–Friday during the season, or catch performances by more mainstream musicians, who also perform here.

Bar Castaneda's Harvey Smashburger honors the Las Vegas hotel's founder, Fred Harvey.

formed (and is ground in-house). The burger features local cheese and local lettuce and local tomatoes (when possible). Purple onion slivers don't overpower but give the burger a slight twang and keep you kissable after. Of course, the chiles are Hatch, and Sinclair even makes his own pickles. Add a secret special sauce, and you've got one heck of a burger, delivered in a foil wrapper with some well-seasoned fries on the side. All of this is made possible in Hotel Castaneda's beautifully renovated dream kitchen, which once served home-cooked meals to weary travelers on the Atchison, Topeka, and Santa Fe Railway when the hotel was a Harvey House, opened in 1898. Sinclair, originally from Tijeras, cut his teeth in Albuquerque and Santa Fe kitchens before bringing the magic here to his Harvey Smash Burger, which earned top honors at the 2019 Green Chile Cheeseburger Smackdown, a prestigious statewide competition held annually in

Santa Fe. (Read about Bar Castaneda's cocktail creations in the wine and spirits chapter.)

GOOD TO KNOW Try the Castaneda's fine-dining restaurant, Kin, which features Sinclair's tasting menu. *524 Railroad Avenue. (505) 434–1005; kinlvnm.com.*

Madrid

Mine Shaft Tavern

What a quirky town Madrid (pronounced "MAD-rid") is. It's situated between Santa Fe and Albuquerque, just a quick trip along a national scenic byway known as the Turquoise Trail. Part mountain hamlet, part artists' enclave, part biker lair, it's been a mining town and a movie set. And through it all, the Mine Shaft Tavern has remained among the central hangouts, primarily due to its surprisingly family-oriented vibe, its hippie atmosphere, and, of course, its green chile cheeseburger, sold here as the Mad Chile Burger. The key ingredient is a combination of chopped green chile and deep-fried chile strips. Then choose your meat: ground Black Angus, New Mexico–grown wagyu beef, veggie, or—here's an unexpected one—locally raised yak. A living version of the long-haired cow relative is the star attraction of Madrid's popular annual Christmas parade, but I'm always surprised to see it on a menu (although folks swear that it tastes even better than bison). The sauce is a chipotle dijonnaise, which is slathered on a Fano Bakery brioche bun, all of which you can enjoy while listening to live music. In the summer, you can check out the adjacent mining museum, filled with old equipment, historic photos, and other glimpses into Madrid's wild past.

GOOD TO KNOW You'll find live performances on weekends as well as other events at the Engine House Theater. *2846 Highway 14. (505) 473–0743; themineshafttavern.com.*

Los Alamos

Pajarito Brewpub and Grill

Los Alamos, home of the mysterious Manhattan Project of the 1940s, is a self-contained community, perched atop the Pajarito Plateau and surrounded by Los Alamos National Laboratory. Visitors come to enjoy the scenery, explore the quirky arts community, and hit the trails at Bandelier National Monument, where Ancestral Puebloans carved out bluff-side homes thousands of years ago. The food scene is somewhat hard to suss out here, but there are delicious pockets if you know where to look. A rewarding meal after climbing the trails and ladders to the dwellings at Bandelier is the Green Chile Pajarito Pub Burger at the Pajarito Brewpub and Grill. Oodles of white cheese and chopped green chile are stuffed inside the New Mexico beef patty, which is then, you guessed it, topped with more green chile. The house-made chips that come with it are crisp and filling, but the truffle fries are worth the extra $2.50. There's also a fine selection of New Mexico and other regional craft beers for the pairing.

GOOD TO KNOW Check out karaoke and trivia nights as well as tap takeovers on select nights. *614 Trinity Drive. (505) 662–8877; pajaritobrewpubandgrill.com.*

Albuquerque

B2B Bistronomy

Vegetarians welcome! When you show up here on a sleepy Albuquerque afternoon, the vibe is distinctly too early for the college crowd and perfectly suited for munching on a burger and sipping a local brew (with more than thirty taps to choose from) while enjoying a healthy dose of Nob Hill people-watching. It's perched right on Central Avenue next to one of the hood's many

B2B Bistronomy's burger comes with a schmear of green chile made with garlic and other spices.

tattoo shops, and I'd almost swear that I was sidewalk dining in a hip neighborhood in Oakland or Portland. The big picture windows open up during good weather, which, let's face it, is most of the time in central New Mexico. And this burger has all the elements of a winner: artisanal buns (emblazoned with a scorched B2B logo), a thick New Mexico–grown Angus patty cooked over a flame, and toppings and sauces that raise the heat and flavor profiles. The New Mexico Burger comes with a choice of red or green sauce (actual sauce and not chopped chiles). I got the red on the side and dipped the fresh-cut, skin-on, twice-fried fries in that ambrosia, although B2B offers four kinds of ketchup and three kinds of mayo for fry dipping. The green chile is more of a schmear: Hatch green chiles pureed with garlic and spices and made into a paste. Vegetarians get their day here too, with options that aren't just meat substitutes but are much more inventive. Take the pecan lentil patty, made from an unlikely smooshing together of nut and legume, bound with parsley, carrots, and radishes. Throw some green chile on that and it's a new day.

GOOD TO KNOW An additional location offers tacos and a brewery at 8338 Comanche Road NE. *3118 Central Avenue SE. (505) 262-2222; b2babq.com.*

The Grill on San Mateo

Part of the draw to this locals' joint is the atmosphere. Owner Phil Chavez chats up customers, delivers free chips and fresh-made salsa, explains all the memorabilia covering the walls (sections are dedicated to law enforcement, military, sports, cowboys, and Hollywood, to name a few), and generally makes folks feel at home. The burger tastes like ones your family cooked up on the backyard Weber—due in large part to the homemade grill that gives the hand-smashed patties just the right amount of char. You decide how you want to dress your burger by visiting the condiment bar, which has the standard offerings as well as the aforementioned chips and salsa. Meat lovers with big families can rejoice at the Giant Burger, which feeds ten people for $100.

The Sacred is Rustic on the Green's elevated green chile cheeseburger offering at Green Jeans Farmery.

GOOD TO KNOW The massive ribeye is popular here, too. *3300 San Mateo Blvd. NE. (505) 872-9772; facebook.com/thegrillonsan mateo.*

Rustic on the Green

When I first explored Green Jeans Food Hall, I believed it to be a mini-universe of eats and treats for hipsters: small outdoor dining spaces, shipping containers turned into gift shops and tasting rooms, a CBD dispensary, dogs and kids hanging out on the small gated patio, a craft brewery (Santa Fe Brewing Company). But it's more than that. It's Albuquerque's little pocket backyard, where everyone can find something they like, from the New Mexico–themed Brotique 505 to a nicely crafted latte at Epiphany Espresso. At Rustic on the Green, the top pick is The Sacred, a sublime ode to the state's venerable green chile cheeseburger. And yes, it has hipster elements— brioche buns from Albuquerque's Fano Bread Company and higher food hall pricing, to name a few. The use of mustard brought an unexpected zing to the party, blending with the American cheese and green chile to form a happy mouthful. The whole delightful package gets even better with the addition of the skinny, crispy fries (extra charge), which are magical with Rustic's green chile dipping sauce (also costs extra). Pair it with a classic IPA from Santa Fe Brewing and, yes, the combo rises to the level of sacred.

GOOD TO KNOW A new location opened at Central Avenue and Tulane in fall 2020. *3600 Cutler Avenue NE. (505) 315-1148; rusticburger505.com.*

Steel Bender Brewyard

Some of us are purists when it comes to our GCCBs, so when you start adding a whole chile relleno and other accoutrement, we get nervous. The signature burger here, The Steel Bender, seems like it might be trying

Steel Bender Brewyard serves a monster of a burger topped with green chile, bacon, and a fried egg.

Pair the Steel Bender Brewyard burgers with a sudsy flight of house or rotating taps.

too hard. They start with house-ground beef, your choice of cheese, and slabs of thick bacon and then pile on a fried egg, a whole fried green chile, and finally the house-made Steel Bender sauce. With all that, you need a bun that can hold up, so popular local bakery Pastian's comes to the rescue with its fluffy but sturdy meat holder. The result? A creation that works together to form an "Oh my gosh" first bite. You'll need two hands and some napkins, but it all holds up, even with the yolk dripping over the beef. I'd recommend splitting this monster, unless you've got a cardiologist on retainer. That way, you can top off with the hand-cut fries and one of the award-winning house-made brewskies or ciders.

GOOD TO KNOW The burger has won several awards, including the 2019 Green Chile Cheeseburger Smackdown. *8305 Second Street NW, Los Ranchos de Albuquerque. (505) 433–3537; steelbenderbrewyard.com.*

TOP PICK

World Famous Laguna Burger

This burger may have turned this die-hard mayo lover into a mustard convert. The mustard on the bun mushes into the green chile to create what could almost be classified as a sharp and spicy new condiment. This sits atop a hand-smashed patty, with just the right amount of char and crispy edges, that peeks out over a buttered, grilled sesame bun. I don't love the iceberg lettuce that sits on it, but I just pluck it off and no one's the wiser. If you've got room after chowing through this two-hander, top off with a side of the nicely greased hand-cut fries or a thick chocolate shake. The atmosphere is authentic here, especially at the two locations on Interstate 40. Locals, many from the nearby Laguna Pueblo, as well as travelers looking for a good meal after a long stretch on Route 66 (known along here as US 40) sit elbow-to-elbow at this often-packed diner–cum–convenience store–cum-souvenir shop.

Laguna Pueblo owns and operates the chain, with three locations. *2400 12th Street NW, Albuquerque; (505) 352–8282. Interstate 40, Exit 140, Rio Puerco; (505) 352–7848. Laguna 66 Pit Stop, Interstate 40, Exit 114, Laguna; (505) 552–7762; thelagunaburger.com.*

San Antonio

Buckhorn Tavern versus the Owl Bar and Café

The burger battle between the Buckhorn Tavern and the Owl Bar and Café has been burning up this tiny town ten miles south of Socorro since the mid-1940s. In my childhood trips to the area, I was not equipped to determine the best burger, but by the time I was in college, making quick

Laguna Pueblo–owned cafés serve up one of the state's best green chile cheeseburgers.

The small town of San Antonio houses two of the state's top burger haunts: Buckhorn Tavern (*top*) and the Owl Bar and Café (*bottom*).

trips from Las Cruces to scope out the abundant birdlife at the Bosque del Apache National Wildlife Refuge, about eight miles south of San Antonio, I'd firmly chosen sides. It's not fair to share, since that was a few decades ago and changes have come. First off, Bobby Flay made an appearance at the Buckhorn in 2009 for his *Throwdown with Bobby Flay* show on the Food Network, and that generated hot publicity for the small eatery. The restaurant temporarily closed in 2019 for a handoff to new owners (who happen to be local chile farmers), but it uses the same well-worn grill and recipe (although I admit that I miss the barroom vibe of yore). The Owl, with its taxidermied owls, beckoning owl mural on its exterior wall, and loyal following, retains a strong GCCB game. The Owl grinds its beef and makes its own "secret" green chile sauce in-house, and while this is a no-frills place packed with character, the burger is tasty and worth the stop. Both have good burgers with hot chile, especially if you're hungry after a day of bosque exploration.

GOOD TO KNOW Both restaurants are closed Sundays. *Owl: 77 US 380. (575) 835–9946; sanantonioowl.com. Buckhorn: 68 US 380. (575) 835–4423; buckhornburgers.com.*

Hatch

TOP PICK

Sparky's Burgers, Barbecue, and Espresso

You might've seen the giant fiberglass rooster on the top of the building. Or the thirty-foot-tall Uncle Sam luring you to join the forces of pepper patriotism. Teako and Josie Nunn, who opened this establishment in 2008 to feed their passions for collecting antiques and serving good food, have managed to create an institution in this small

Sparky's, located in the heart of Hatch's green chile fields, keeps its burger recipe simple: meat, cheese, chile, and bun.

farming community, where the heart of chile beats hot and green. The former mercantile buildings have been repurposed with advertising signs and other cool ephemera, but the star here is the green chile cheeseburger. It's a simple affair: a patty flavored with the "family seasoning," a slice of cheddar, a healthy heaping of fresh-from-the-field chile (fall is harvest time), and a super-soft bun. "Just meat, cheese, bun, and green chile," Teako says with pride. It all mushes together to make burger magic. On the side you can get pineapple coleslaw, pinto beans, or sweet corn with Hatch green chile and onion, but the batter-dipped and deep-fried potato wedges are the prime accompaniment. Feeling the burn? A vanilla shake is an antidote for a hot tongue, or you can amp up the heat by ordering the green chile shake. Come early or after peak hours; lines form out the front door. Live bands draw folks from all over the area.

GOOD TO KNOW Closed Monday through Wednesday. *115 Franklin Street. (575) 267–4222; sparkysburgers.com.*

Las Cruces

Chachi's Mexican Restaurant

This low-key establishment has two locations, both with a Mexican beach vibe with hand-carved chairs and brightly painted tables. The Chachi's Burger is a certified two-hander, with a patty that overlaps the buttered and grilled bun. The creamy guacamole inside is the glue that binds two strips of thick smoky bacon, which form crosshairs on the meat and play well with the green chile's strong burn. There's a lot going on here, but it's worth the pile of napkins you'll leave behind. A note of caution: The free chips and salsa are local favorites and can induce a pre-meal feeding frenzy.

GOOD TO KNOW Chachi's Express on Locust Street offers drive-through and order pickup. *2460 S. Locust Street, Las Cruces. (575) 522–7322; 505 Joe Gutierrez Street, Doña Ana. (575) 652–3071. chachis-lc.com.*

The house-smoked bacon elevates the burger at Chala's Wood Fire Grill in Las Cruces.

Chala's Wood Fire Grill

Who knew smoked meats could take the GCCB to such great heights? Apparently, the folks behind Chala's do, as they smoke their own bacon and other pork for their carnivore-friendly menu. The A-Mountain Burger (named for the hill marked for the Aggies of New Mexico State University) is a superb creation with a perfectly cooked char-grilled patty, a layer of cheddar covering a hot scoop of chopped green chile, and a loop of purple onion, all cooled with a romaine leaf and a ripe tomato slice. The meat is so juicy that no mayo or ketchup is required. Two thick pieces of bacon poke out from the bun and add a smokiness that will make your eyes roll back in your head with every bite. Need a burger break? Try the tacos al pastor or the Hefty Cuban (made with house-smoked pork and bacon). Pair it all with a New Mexico–brewed IPA, and the euphoria is complete. Worth noting is that on weekends, Chala's modifies its signature to form a popular brunch burger topped with an egg and green chile jam.

GOOD TO KNOW The pastor tacos are a close second to the burgers here. *2790 Avenida de Mesilla. (575) 652–4143.*

Peppers, Mesilla

Peppers is the casual courtyard dining room inside the posh Double Eagle Restaurant, one of the food anchors on the small but mighty Mesilla Plaza. Located in one of the oldest buildings on the plaza, a two-room house built in 1849 in what was then the Mexican village of Mesilla, the restaurant not surprisingly has resident ghosts, star-crossed lovers who like to linger in the Carlotta Salon. The Mesilla Green Chile Cheeseburger features a half-pound char-broiled patty that tastes as though it came off a charcoal grill and is a hearty partner to the green chile sauce generously dolloped on top and bookended by a toasted brioche

Peppers brings the heat with its Mesilla Green Chile Cheeseburger, made with a half-pound patty and topped with a thick roasted green chile.

The Hillsboro General Store Café serves a side of history with its juicy burgers.

bun. Or order the relleno-topped version, which adds a crispy layer between the meat and bun. (Read more about the Double Eagle in the margaritas chapter.)

GOOD TO KNOW The menu features the World's Largest Green Chile Cheeseburger, twenty-four ounces, for $32.95. *2355 Calle de Guadalupe. (575) 523–6700; doubleeagle online.com.*

Hillsboro

Hillsboro General Store Café

Travelers en route to Silver City to explore the Gila Wilderness might be tempted to drive right through Hillsboro. But this is the perfect place to stop, before traversing fifty-seven miles of windy switchbacks, to take stock of the beauty and history of this area. Here massive trees shade buildings dating to the 1800s, seemingly paused in time. The Hillsboro General Store, which occupies a mercantile dating to 1879, has been repurposed as a restaurant that also sells merchandise and serves some old-fashioned hospitality along with a killer green chile cheeseburger. As at any respectable New Mexican restaurant, diners receive complimentary chips and salsa—in this case, chips right out of the fryer and delivered warm. The burger has almost a meat loaf flavor and texture, which is made even meatier with a slice of bacon. The chile is mild, but the meat takes up most of the flavor profile. The fries hold their own here—the potatoes are fresh-cut with the skins on and deep-fried to crisp perfection. (Read the sweets chapter to learn about the restaurant's bumbleberry pie.)

GOOD TO KNOW The store and the restaurant are for sale, so call ahead and make sure they're open if you're making the trip. *10697 Highway 152. (575) 895–5306; facebook.com/hillsborogeneralstorecafe.*

Deming

Mama Fats Burgers and Ice Cream

I know I'm just supposed to talk about green chile cheeseburgers here, but I'd be remiss to leave out Mama Fats's Zipper Ripper, a monster that has folks making the sixty-mile drive from Las Cruces to chow down on it. The Zipper starts with two flavorful patties and then piles on a fried avocado wedge, a fried green tomato, and a stack of fried onions (and bacon, of course), which are all glued to the bun with a gooey slice of Havarti. This burger is sharable, but I'd suggest taking a friend who can order the Classic New Mexico, a concoction that is a bit more manageable but provides the necessary dose of green chile (this creation is taken up a notch with a dollop of guac). The options here make me want to continue to try new things: the Cherry Chingon features a beef and chorizo patty topped with a fried egg, maple bacon, and cherry aioli, and there's a Sonoran dog for the homesick Arizonans.

GOOD TO KNOW Top off with a hand-scooped milkshake in multiple flavors. *1521 Columbus Road. (575) 546–9888; mamafatsnm.com.*

Alamogordo

Rockin' BZ Burgers

The Champ, a New Mexico State Fair Centennial Green Chile Cheeseburger Challenge winner in 2012, is still a big winner around these parts. Made with half a pound of ground beef (or you can opt for the quarter-pound version), this monster has onions and spices cooked inside the meat, making it one of the tastiest patties in the state. The patty is embraced by two slices of cheese and then topped with lettuce, tomatoes, grilled onions, and a healthy spoonful of hot Hatch green chile, all on a doughy

The aptly named Champ at Rockin' BZ Burgers is Alamogordo's top chomp.

sourdough bun. A rather nondescript building on the north end of Alamogordo houses this burger haven, but it does feature large picture windows framing views of the Sacramento Mountains. BZ, which opened in 2012, rivals the other top burger contender in town, Hi-D-Ho Drive In, home of the Tiger Burger, named for Alamogordo's high school mascot.

GOOD TO KNOW Rockin' BZ is closed Mondays, and Hi-D-Ho is open daily. *Rockin BZ: 3005 N. White Sands Blvd. (575) 434–2375. Hi-D-Ho: 414 White Sands Blvd. (575) 437–6400. facebook.com/hidhodrivein.*

Cloudcroft

Mad Jack's Mountaintop Barbecue

New Mexicans aren't necessarily accustomed to standing in line for barbecue. But everyone waiting in the smoky aromas wafting out of this two-story clapboard building will tell you that the meat is worth the wait. The brisket is the magnum opus, smoked over wood hauled in from the owners' hometown of Lockhart, Texas. My

Mad Jack's Mountaintop Barbecue in Cloudcroft mixes its famed wood-smoked brisket with green chile to deliver one of the state's best sandwiches.

The green chile cheeseburgers at Ruidoso's Hall of Flame are worth the wait.

favorite pairing is the Chile the Kid sandwich (a glorious combination of chopped brisket with Hatch green chile) with the sour cream potato salad. (The bacon-flecked mac and cheese is also hard to beat.)

GOOD TO KNOW Come early to beat the rush and to ensure the restaurant doesn't run out of your favorites (which it often does). *105 James Canyon Highway. (575) 682–7577; facebook.com/madjacksbbqshack.*

Ruidoso

TOP PICK

Hall of Flame Burgers

The last time I dropped by this Ruidoso favorite, it was the middle of the afternoon. The line snaked out into the mini-mall where this restaurant resides and curled down the sidewalk. As soon as I got close enough to see the cash register, the aroma of chiles hit my nose. As I waited for my burger, I watched the cooks managing the flames on the open grill and flipping patties in the kitchen, the centerpiece of the dining room. By the time my burger got to me in its little basket, I thought there was no way it could live up to the anticipation. But it did. Buttery buns hold together this concoction, which includes an oversize square patty, a slab of green chile, tomato, purple onion, and a small handful of shredded iceberg lettuce. The fries are dusted with a delicate seasoning of parmesan, salt, and herbs, and, yes, you can add green chile to those. From my table, I could see all the people standing in line, anticipating the same joys I was experiencing, and I didn't feel one ounce of guilt about it.

GOOD TO KNOW As noted, this place gets busy, especially on weekends. Arrive at 11 a.m. opening time to beat the rush. *2500 Sudderth Drive. (575) 257–9987.*

A famous bear and an award-winning burger keep customers happy at Oso Grill in scenic Capitan.

TOP PICK

Oso Grill, Capitan

Top Pick: Welcome to Smokey Bear's hometown. (*Oso* is Spanish for "bear.") This primo burger stopover is just one highlight of this little mountain burg, where you can work up an appetite strolling through Smokey Bear Historical Park to learn about the famed US Forest Service mascot, take a few selfies with the Smokey statues, pause to smell the wildflowers, and then pay respects at the bear's final resting place. My parents brought me here when there was not much more than a stone marker, so this is high-level nostalgia for me and others who grew up loving the little bear cub who was rescued in 1950 by a ranger following a fire in the Capitan Mountains. Smokey became our nation's living symbol of forest fire prevention, and he was my hero. Visitors come here to learn about Smokey and another famous former resident, Billy the Kid, an Old West outlaw and a participant in New Mexico's Lincoln County War. But people also come here to enjoy one of the state's finest green chile cheeseburgers. And this one is a whopper (not that kind): a juicy hand-formed patty, cradled between two pieces of American cheese, topped with both diced chile and chile strips deep-fried in a delicate batter. The slightly sweet bun is fresh and holds up under the pressure. This burger won the Green Chile Cheeseburger Challenge at the New Mexico State Fair two years in a row. I think Smokey would approve.

GOOD TO KNOW Closed Sundays and Mondays. *100 Lincoln Avenue. (575) 354–2327; facebook.com/osogrillcapitan.*

A bug-eyed party greets humanoids at Roswell's International UFO Museum and Research Center.

While You're Here: Roswell

INTERNATIONAL UFO MUSEUM AND RESEARCH CENTER Something happened in the desert near Roswell in 1947 that left an indelible mark on this remote community. Some claim a UFO crashed and that interplanetary beings were found at the site. The government issued different accounts. Either way, the story has captured the imagination of the public for decades and the "Roswell Incident" is still being studied and debated. This museum takes the incident, and accounts of those who were there at the time, seriously and then allows visitors to attempt to unravel the mysteries themselves. Roswell isn't shy about its UFO history—those bug-eyed little green men statues and images all over town make for great selfies—and this museum offers a compelling and detailed look at the effects of UFO-mania on this town and our culture in general. *roswellufomuseum.com.*

ANDERSON MUSEUM OF CONTEMPORARY ART Wow. With all the bulgy-eyed green man kitsch that dominates here, you might forget that beneath it beats the heart of a strong arts community that was here before the spaceships arrived. Established by local philanthropist Don Anderson, this museum houses works of those who've participated in the Roswell Artist-in-Residence Program over a span of more than forty years, bringing unique perspectives and world-class creations to this small town. The rambling, cavernous museum houses more than five hundred contemporary works tucked into twelve galleries, with pieces ranging from giant fiberglass sculptures to ceramics to mixed media. *rair.org.*

Roswell

Chef Toddzilla's Gourmet Burgers and Mobile Cuisine

I have a complicated relationship with food trucks. Maybe it's the long lines or the juggle I am forced to perform as I struggle to hold my flimsy paper bowl of food while the wind blows my napkin away. What I do love about food trucks is that they've become a platform for creative chefs and food entrepreneurs—who may not be ready for a brick-and-mortar commitment—to try things and stretch those culinary muscles. Food trucks have also made space for devotees of specialized genres, such as gourmet grilled cheese, ice cream sandwiches, and, perhaps most famously, fusion tacos. Fortunately, some food trucks get to park permanently, so you don't have to follow them on Twitter just to find lunch. Chef Todd Alexander and his partner and wife, Kerry, started in a food truck dedicated to burgers and in 2017 put it in park to open a small open-air eatery that attracts fans, be it cold and rainy or blisteringly hot. I still have to chase napkins across the parking lot, but I know I can count on that Zilla Cheeseburger, a honking mess of a sandwich made with a bacon–beef mixture and topped with fried green chile, a tangy pico de gallo, and, if you so desire, a smear of garlic mayo or baconnaise. Opt for the double and share that monster. You can choose between the regular 505 Green Chile Cheeseburger and the chorizo version, which incorporates two kinds of pork into house-ground beef, which is then

ROSWELL MUSEUM AND ART CENTER
This museum opened 1937, a decade before aliens even knew Roswell existed. With its well-curated exhibits and twelve galleries, the museum is the cultural heart of the city. If you're still stuck on space stuff, the museum's Goddard Planetarium offers films dedicated to the stars and science in its high-tech domed theater. *roswell-nm .gov/308/roswell-museum-art-center.*

DOWNTOWN ROSWELL This town is an interesting mix of alien-based attractions, intriguing architecture, and military history, so it's worthwhile to take a stroll and soak it all in. Pick up the free Roswell walking tour map; highlights include the Roswell UFO Spacewalk (a blacklight walk-through attraction); alien-themed gift shops such as Alien Invasion; a UFO-shaped McDonald's; the imposing green-domed Chaves County Courthouse, built in 1911; and the equally imposing New Mexico Military Institute, which houses a military museum and its own art collections.

OUTDOORS The scenic red bluffs of nearby Bottomless Lakes State Park make for excellent boating, fishing, and splashing. Birdwatchers train their binoculars on the migrating waterfowl that congregate at Bitter Lake National Wildlife Refuge, a series of sinkholes that attract a range of critters, from dragonflies and salamanders to ospreys and owls. Feeling sporty? From May through July you can catch a Roswell Invaders baseball game and pick up some cool swag. (The team, part of the Pecos League and not affiliated with a professional league, wears bright green uniforms and is fun to watch.)

shmooshed with red chile. You can get either in bowl form rather than with buns, if you prefer. The best news is that burger prices (around $9) include cut-when-you-order, perfectly crisped fries, which can be a meal unto themselves with a chorizo patty and a fried egg, among other options. The seasonal Cheesecake Bomb, a tortilla-wrapped flash-fried cheesecake, made it

into an episode of *Pizza Masters* on the Cooking Channel in 2014. Wash it all down with one of several colorful lemonade and exotic fountain drink options, such as the AbducTEA.

GOOD TO KNOW Closed Sundays and Mondays. *107 Twin Diamond Road. (575) 755–3663; cheftoddzilla.com.*

5 Two Roads
Green and Red

It's not as divisive as *Star Wars* versus *Star Trek*, or snowboarders versus skiers, or UNM Lobos versus NMSU Aggies, but it's an important distinction that's always at the heart of any New Mexican food menu: red or green?

I consider New Mexico to be lucky in that regard. During the many years I enjoyed Californian and southern cuisine, I was never once asked that question, even in areas where the cuisine yielded tamales and enchiladas. Even in Mexico, Texas, and Arizona, the question rarely comes up. So it does my heart good to be asked to consider whether to have my tortillas and cheese slathered in a rich, roasty red sauce or a spicy, peppery green one.

For me, the answer is almost always Christmas, so I can taste the kitchen's interpretation of both. Sometimes the red stands out, melding with cheese or pork with a salty warmth that, when you finish your meal, sits right next to your heart. Sometimes the green takes center stage—its sharp mouth burn and green pepper flavor scratching a deep itch on the palate.

When I introduce newcomers to New Mexico chile culture, I have to coach them on this question. In the process, I also discover that I don't always have answers for why we do things the way we do them when it comes to consuming chile. A conversation might go like this:

Red? Green? Both?
Depends on the place.
The red is tops at the Baca
Boys Café in Albuquerque.

PEPPER APPRENTICE: What should I order?

PEPPER PROFESSIONAL (me): Combo, and try to pick one with a chile relleno (unless it's winter, in which case it's a traditional time to enjoy a tamale).

PA: Red or green?

PP: [smiles] Christmas.

PA: So the stuff that's made with red or green chile also has both red and green chile on it? How does that work?

PP: I don't know; it's just how we do it. We also eat too many chips and salsa before the meal comes. It's just how it's done.

Thusly, we both walk out full of all forms of chile that have been poured on top of chile-filled things. And no matter how full we are, we finish with a sopaipilla slathered in honey. It's just how it's done.

The other refrain I hear often from out-of-towners is: "New Mexicans put chile on everything." It's true. It's on our pizzas, burgers, and eggs. It's in our bread, beer, milkshakes, and chocolate. At Thanksgiving, red chile stands in as our gravy. It's on the menu at McDonald's and Wendy's, and a friend of mine boycotts Five Guys because the fast-food chain has locations in New Mexico yet refuses to add green chile to its list of burger toppings.

In short, to a New Mexican, whether it's a burger patty or a corn tortilla, it's all just a chile delivery system designed to provide the fix. The good news is that because of New Mexico's passion for the pepper, eateries put all their love into their reds and greens, and when you're biting into a plate of gloopy enchiladas, you're tasting our heritage, our agriculture, and our talent for bringing the heat.

Of course, the challenge on this New Mexican–centric food trail is that while recipes might remain somewhat consistent across kitchens, those reds and greens can vary by heat and intensity of flavor. So while one day you might love a restaurant's green chile, the next week the red might be the better option. And during chile harvest season, a relatively short period starting in late July and extending through September, you can almost always count on the green being fresh—so place your chile order accordingly. Because, as a rule, we do put chile on everything, the goal in this chapter is to guide you to some of the state's unique and most flavorful places for sorting your reds and greens.

Farmington

The Chile Pod

Variety is the spice of life, right? I therefore present The Chile Pod Dip. Each bite consists of a mouthful of savory tender beef, crispy fried onions, and creamy white cheese, all in a toasted hoagie and topped with a tinge of hot diced green chile. I didn't care that I had juice dripping down my chin, even when the waitress came by to refill my iced tea. And here's the catch: Rather than a traditional au jus made from drippings, a side of red chile is there for the dipping. And dipping you'll do. That stuff is like red crack. In fact, owner-chef Monica Shultz has won several cook-off awards for her red chile—so many that one local authority told me people stopped entering competitions in which she was a participant. All the New Mexican dishes are worth sampling, including the red chile–

At the Chile Pod in Farmington, the Chile Pod Dip is topped with green chile, with a side of red for dipping.

smothered New Mexican Burger (the green chile is worthy too).

GOOD TO KNOW Check the schedule here for local musicians as well as painting classes. *121 W. Main Street. (505) 258-4585; cravethechilepod.com.*

Española

El Paragua

My first "food high" occurred about fifteen years ago when I was living in Los Angeles, following a superb meal at the legendary Roscoe's Chicken and Waffles. The second? A combination plate at El Paragua. I remember it as if it were yesterday: We were driving through New Mexico and decided to stop here for a bite on a late spring afternoon. We were ahead of the dinner rush, so the restaurant was bustling but not crowded. As my eyes adjusted to the indoor light, I noticed a massive elm growing inside near the bar. "That's a good start," I thought. I ordered a house margarita and perused the menu of New Mexican and Mexican fare: posole, enchiladas, chicken tacos. I pieced together a combo that consisted of enchiladas, a chile relleno, and some other stuff and tucked in. We were New Mexico natives who'd been away from our homeland for a decade or so, and this meal brought back everything I loved about New Mexico comfort food. The red chile of the enchilada looked like a rich red fabric speckled with grated yellow cheese and onions. I dug through to the relleno, which had gotten lost in sauce. As I slurped the remaining margarita from the ice in my glass, we finished with poufy sopaipillas that we smeared with house-made apricot jam. It was then that a warmth spread through my chest—and it wasn't just the margarita. My face glowed, and I wore an irrepressible smile.

I am not alone in my love for this

rock-constructed restaurant that started out as a humble taco stand in 1966. Famous faces have left autographs and sketches on the walls, and a few haughty publications, such as the *New York Times* and *Bon Appétit*, have issued high-praising reviews. El Paragua's popularity means that the prices are on the high side, but you might pay anything to chase that food high.

GOOD TO KNOW Dinner entrées are in the $14–$26 range. El Paragua also owns six northern New Mexico locations of the more budget-friendly El Parasol, one of the best places to fill up on such New Mexican food staples as tacos, breakfast burritos, Frito pie, tamales, and green chile cheeseburgers. *603 Santa Cruz Road. (505) 753–3211; elparagua.com.*

Taos

La Cueva Café

This tiny eatery has scarcely enough room to seat the average family and a few extended relatives, yet that doesn't deter most of us from pursuing the area's best ceviche and seafood enchiladas. The chicken mole enchiladas here are rich and meaty too, as is the green mole pork, which unexpectedly ignites the taste buds of jaded New Mexican palates. The flan also gets high marks for being *auténtico*, and the rich Mexican chocolate cake will make your eyes roll back in your head.

GOOD TO KNOW Beat the rush by hitting up this place for breakfast (try the Enchiladas de Huevo con Mole Poblano). *135 Paseo del Pueblo Sur. (575) 758–7001; lacuevacafe .com.*

opposite On special nights, Doc Martin's at the Taos Inn serves its legendary green chile stew.

Doc Martin's Restaurant, Taos Inn

Ready to warm up? The legendary Doc Martin's at the Taos Inn near Taos Plaza has a hearty green chile stew that will heat your insides and fill you up for the day. Everything on this menu is worth the stop— chiles rellenos, the green chile cheeseburger, the Chimayó red chile–marinated carne asada—but Abuelito's Green Chile Pork Stew is my numero uno (offered seasonally and as an occasional special, so call ahead if you're counting on it). The chile is fiery, the pork delivered in big and flavorful chunks, and the veggies hearty; a drizzle of heavy cream on top eases the chile burn. Combined with a Cowboy Buddha Margarita, this stew offers the perfect topper to a day of hiking or skiing at the legendary Taos Ski Valley. (Read more in the margaritas chapter.)

GOOD TO KNOW Doc Martin's is the restaurant tucked inside the Taos Inn, known as the "Living Room of Taos," where guests come to meet up and listen to live local music nightly except Mondays. *125 Paseo del Pueblo Norte. (575) 425–0169; taosinn.com.*

Orlando's New Mexican Café

"If you're headed to Taos, you have to eat at Orlando's." You'll hear that across the board if you ask where to grab a meal in this northern New Mexico mountain town. And those folks aren't wrong. Filling this tidy adobe casa are bright murals, Mexican rustic furniture, and tile-topped tables. The vibe is hometown, *abuela*-style cooking, and both the green and red chile are worth the drive. If you want a sampling, go with the Los Colores Plate, which provides a green chicken enchilada, a red beef enchilada, and a cheese Caribe enchilada. They all play well together, but you might want to start with the lighter red before you go Caribe, which is a pure, deep red sauce made straight from the red pods (and not

Red and green are standard options with the Los Colores Plate at Orlando's New Mexican Café in Taos.

powder). You can taste the terroir and the warmth of the sun in the chile, and the sauce gives the enchiladas heft. You have a choice of sides, but posole is the way to go. (Read about their famed avocado pie in the sweets chapter.)

GOOD TO KNOW Closed on Sundays. *1114 Don Juan Valdez Lane. (575) 751–1450; facebook.com/orlandosnewmexicancafe.*

Santa Fe

Cafe Pasqual's

Plan ahead if you want to dine at this Santa Fe institution, which has been serving locals and visitors just off the plaza for the past forty years. The small restaurant doesn't take reservations for breakfast or lunch, and you have to wait outside, but the experience is worth it. Breakfast, lunch, and dinner menus revolve around classic Mexican, New Mexican, and Asian flavors, with executive chef and owner Katharine Kagel bringing a creative and ingenious twist to each of her dishes (which you can try to emulate by picking up San Pasqual's popular cookbooks

at the restaurant). For lunch, the mole enchiladas is my go-to dish. Long after I leave, I continue to daydream about that rich red sauce and how it plays with the tender chunks of chicken and blue corn tortillas. For breakfast, go with the huevos barbacoa, a hearty dish with tender beef cheeks that melt in the mouth when combined with the egg yolks, corn tortillas, and red arbol chile sauce. The dining room is also a gallery, with murals and other artwork displayed on walls and in every nook and cranny, all curated by Kagel.

GOOD TO KNOW Known primarily as a breakfast or lunch spot, Pasqual's is also open for dinner, but reservations are recommended. An online store sells T-shirts, tea towels, cookies, and other treats. *121 Don Gaspar Avenue. (505) 983–9340; pasquals.com.*

The huevos barbacoa swim in a delectable red chile at Café Pasqual's, a Santa Fe dining institution.

TOP PICK

The Shed

Wandering the streets around the Santa Fe Plaza, you're likely to feel as though you've been dropped into a time capsule. Adobe buildings dating back to the 1600s line the narrow streets, where visitors amble along uneven sidewalks and low-hanging portals, giving Santa Fe an authentic, romantic charm. While meandering, you'll undoubtedly spot the crowd milling about outside The Shed, a cozy and delightfully rambling and brightly colored hacienda with low-slung doorways behind a patio on Palace Street. You might be tempted to find another restaurant with a shorter wait time, but if you can hang, the New Mexican fare here is legendary. I would sell my soul for a bite of that posole any day of the week. Rather than being served in a bowl, it comes as a side to your meal, happily mixing all juices with your entrée. If I were forced to order something besides my beloved blue corn enchiladas, Christmas, with a fried egg on top, I'd go with the chicken enchiladas as a close second. Rather than tortillas, The Shed serves a side of buttery garlic bread to sop up the remaining chile on your plate, a tradition the restaurant has had since it first began serving folks from its original location in Burro Alley in the 1950s.

GOOD TO KNOW The wait times are long, and reservations are accepted for dinner only. But you can swing by when it opens (11 a.m.; closed on Sundays), put your name on the list, and then take a plaza walk while you wait. The same great food and chile are served at its sister restaurant, La Choza, located near the Railyard. The website store sells spices, salsas, and, my favorite, a posole kit. *113 1/2 E. Palace Avenue. (505) 982–9030; sfshed.com.*

Christmas is the way to go at Tia Sophia's, which is credited with creating the term that means having both colors of chile on the same dish.

TOP PICK

Tia Sophia's

The late Jim Maryol, who founded this restaurant in 1975, might not have invented breakfast burritos—after all, he noted that New Mexicans had been putting eggs and chile into tortillas for longer than we all can recall—but he certainly was among the first in this region to put a breakfast burrito on the menu. And what a fine version it is. This baby is made with a fresh flour tortilla stuffed with scrambled eggs, your choice of meat, and chunky potatoes, all slathered with red or green chile. It's one of New Mexico's purest, most basic comfort foods, and here they do it better than just about anyone else. The green chile is thick and stewy and has that deep pepper flavor that chile lovers chase. The red is tangy and textured. All the ingredients are good on their own, but when you combine them, they are

The carne adovada enchiladas might be the star at Baca Boys Café, but the rice and calabacitas hold their own.

greater than the sum of their parts. Is there a secret ingredient in the red or green sauce? Nah, just "time and love," says Jim's son, Nicholas Maryol, who now oversees the restaurant. Oh, and making the chile in small batches using Hatch peppers. Then, he says, "it's just a big pot with chile and garlic."

GOOD TO KNOW Waitress Martha Rotuno, who worked here in the 1980s, first used the term *Christmas* to mean both red and green chile on the same dish. *210 W. San Francisco Street. (505) 983–9880; tiasophias.com.*

Albuquerque

Baca Boys Café

Local eateries like this are what make me wish I lived in Albuquerque, or at least that I could get there quicker. The food hits the spot in the best New Mexico way, the atmosphere is easy and inviting despite being close to the bustle of downtown, and it can work both as your favorite breakfast and lunch spot. Meat lovers can lean into the carne adovada enchiladas, a good all-day filler (Christmas, of course, since both types of chile are superb). Served on the side, the calabacitas (a traditional squash dish) are roasty and flavorful, and the rice is among the best in New Mexico. (I gobbled up mine before I even started on my main dish.) Caution: The chips and salsa are made in-house and are therefore addicting, so you'll probably eat too many. But you can always pack up lunch for leftovers later.

GOOD TO KNOW Open daily till 3 p.m. *102 Fourth Street NW. (505) 200–0065.*

Barelas Coffee House

This always-packed, no-frills mom-and-pop joint has fed former presidents, a slew of local politicos, and a range of other visitors seeking an authentic local food experience in this historic South Valley neighborhood. A glimpse at the menu reveals pervasive Mexican and New Mexican influences: menudo, house-made tortillas, a bowl of beans worth ordering by itself (with a dash of green chile, of course), and a carne adovada and eggs dish that delivers a red chile–tender pork bite that melts in your mouth. The chicharrones—chunks of pork belly that are boiled and then fried to a crispy but tender consistency—can be ordered as a side or on a burrito. But if you love them, try them in the red enchiladas—a magical combination of rich red chile melding with strong pork flavors that evokes the singing of angels.

GOOD TO KNOW This place gets packed around noon, so aim for morning or early afternoon before it closes at 3 p.m. *1502 Fourth Street SW; (505) 843-7577; facebook .com/thebarelascoffeehouse.*

Casa de Benavidez New Mexican Restaurant

A few years ago I took a cruise that docked in Ensenada, where we, among many other passengers, ambled off the ship to explore the sleepy tourist town. Every shop and eatery we entered was eager to please, with on-the-spot service, lush outdoor seating among a variety of flowering plants, and pretty darned good food. Casa de Benavidez reminds me of those places in Mexico, where the margaritas are smooth, the clientele mellow, and the gurgling of the outdoor waterfall evokes a vacation vibe, all of it without being touristy. Hector Pimentel, an Albuquerque master guitarist from the famed luthier family, provides weekend entertainment, further putting diners in an "I've escaped from daily life" mode. The food here doesn't knock me out, but I do appreciate that they take the chile relleno game up a notch by incorporating chicken and beefing up the batter on the chile. Plus, the forty-year-old restaurant was one of the first to offer a sopaipilla burger, which was a big hit when owners Paul and Rita Benavidez first served it out of a tiny carryout eatery nearby before moving to their current, rambling adobe. The poufy sopes on their own are worth the trip and are the perfect accompaniment to the margs, music, and tropical patio—no cruise required.

GOOD TO KNOW The Casa's popular breakfast menu is available daily till noon and all day on Sundays (along with Bloody Marys). *8032 Fourth Street NW; (505) 897-7493. casadebenavidez.com.*

El Patio de Albuquerque

Native New Mexicans make only a few demands when it comes to their chile, but they are important ones. "For enchiladas, the chile doesn't need any additional spices except for salt," says a native New Mexican friend who's made more pots of red chile in her kitchen than any of us can imagine. In that red vein, one of her favorite places is El Patio: "They use real red chile," meaning it's made from pods, with no powder or spices to muck up the pure essence and heat of the fruit. The red enchiladas offer the right balance of cheese and onions, and I recommend a fried egg on top. I also like that instead of rice, the plates come with chunky home fries, a better mechanism for soaking up the extra sauce. Surprisingly (or maybe not, given her skills at making red chile at home), my friend favors the green chile chicken enchiladas. With their zing and strong chile flavor, they've had a loyal following since the restaurant opened near the University of New Mexico in 1977. As with any New Mexican restaurant worth its salt, entrees come with a side of sopaipillas, suitable for chile cleanup or honey-dribbling.

GOOD TO KNOW While locals tend to favor the original location in Nob Hill near UNM, a second location serves the folks near Old Town and also has outdoor seating (nice for sipping margaritas in the fresh air). *142 Harvard Drive SE; (505) 268–4245; 3851 Rio Grande NW; (505) 433–4499. elpatioabq.com.*

High Noon Restaurant and Saloon

A friend of mine has the perfect Friday afternoon routine: Get a haircut at the nearby barbershop in Old Town, then saunter into this neat little historic adobe restaurant for a New Mexico–brewed beer and a plate of High Noon's red chile beef bites. My friend is a hard-core carnivore, so when

Carnivores rejoice at the High Noon Restaurant and Saloon, where the red chile beef bites are popular.

he recommends a meat dish, I get myself there posthaste. And I'm glad I did. The beef bites are on the starters side of the menu, but I guarantee you will not leave hungry. These tenderloin beef chunks are cured in coriander, brown sugar, shallots, and salt and pepper, then given a light coating of flour before being flash-fried to a slight crisp. They then go into a sumptuous red chile butter bath and are delivered to you with a side of tortillas, like edible paper towels for wiping up the leftover sauce. The specialty here is meat, so you can't go wrong with the braised short rib or the pulled pork sandwich either, and the green chile wagyu beef burger is another showstopper. Pair that with a choice of more than thirty tequilas—and maybe a haircut—and you've got the perfect afternoon in Old Town. (Read more in the margaritas chapter.)

GOOD TO KNOW Originally built as a home in the mid-1700s, this rambling structure has also served as a gambling hall and brothel, a home and storefront for a furniture maker, and an apartment for a nun. Yes, it is said to be haunted. *425 San Felipe Avenue NW. (505) 765–1455; highnoonrestaurant.com.*

Mary and Tito's Café

No matter what you order at this Albuquerque institution, get the red. Huevos rancheros? Red. Blue corn enchiladas? Yep, red. Mexican turnovers stuffed with carne adovada? Again, go with the red. The green is good, but the red here has a flavor and texture that all New Mexicans chase whenever they order a combo. The carne adovada has achieved legendary status, and diners have multiple options for how they can receive it: in enchiladas, in a flauta, or as a pizza, among others.

GOOD TO KNOW Folks here also swear by the Mexican wedding cake, but I've always been too full to try it (since the

Let's Talk Frito Pie

Its origins are hotly debated—although I'm not sure who really wants to claim the title as the first to dump chili and chile inside a Frito bag—but nevertheless, it's a "dish" that has legs in New Mexico. And for good reason: Our state's red chile stands up to the salty-corny Fritos, which soak up the juices to create their own umami. Frito pie fans flock to the Santa Fe Plaza's Five & Dime General Store. This tourist shop with a snack bar has been featured on several food and travel shows, including Anthony Bourdain's *Parts Unknown*. You'll find Frito pies on the menu at numerous cafés around the state, and they're always affordable and delicious. Others that get rave reviews come from El Parasol, which has six northern New Mexico locations owned by El Paragua of Española, El Farolito in tiny El Rito north of Española, and Sugar's BBQ in Embudo (thirty-seven miles southwest of Taos), which offers a version made with brisket.

chips and salsa are complimentary). *2711 Fourth Street NW. (505) 344–6266; maryandtitoscafeabq.com.*

Sadie's of New Mexico

My go-to at this Albuquerque staple is almost always the chiles rellenos. The thick cornmeal batter (made with Bosque Brewing beer) maintains its crispness and helps the chile hold its shape under the weight of the red or green chile on top. And the salsa, a perfect marriage of tomato twang and chile kick, has led to many the feeding frenzy, especially when paired with the fresh-from-the-fryer salty corn chips. I tend to favor the green here, but Sadie's enchiladas in either red or green (or both) scratch a special New Mexican comfort food itch, especially when you add spicy ground beef or the slow-cooked brisket. Sadie's loves to pile on the cheese, which helps cut the burn of the chile but can fill you up quicker (especially when you've overdone it on the aforementioned chips and salsa). My advice? Take your time and explore this menu via multiple visits. Each item represents a favorite dish that folks have returned to since the place first opened in the 1970s.

GOOD TO KNOW Thankfully, Sadie's Salsa is available by the jar at grocery stores throughout the United States as well as at sadiessalsa.com. *6230 Fourth Street NW, Los Ranchos de Albuquerque; (505) 345–5339. 15 Hotel Circle NE; (505) 296–6940. 5400 Academy Road NE; (505) 821–9034. sadiesofnew mexico.com.*

Las Cruces

TOP PICK

Chope's Bar and Café, La Mesa

Chope's is the heart of southern New Mexican cuisine. It all started in 1915 in an old adobe in La Mesa, a tiny farming community about twenty miles southeast of Las Cruces, where local resident Longina Benavides started cooking enchiladas with her own sauce and handmade tortillas for area farmers and workhands. When Longina's daughter-in-law Guadalupe married Jose "Chope" Benavides in 1937, she took over the kitchen and incorporated her recipes, adding tamales and what would become her famous chiles rellenos. Chope and Guadalupe were a beacon of home-cooking and

Chope's Bar and Café in Las Mesa serves as a top spot for regional cuisine.

social life for locals, including to one person of particular importance to me: my mom. A young Cora Justice had moved to the La Mesa area from Indiana and married a young farmer there. (She was later widowed and went on to marry my dad, from Hatch.) Chope's was one of the places where she traded her midwestern palate for a Mexican one. I have no doubt that my mom's love for

spicy Mexican food—and her ability to whip up some of the best enchiladas in Las Cruces—came from her life in La Mesa. Today, I can taste the same red and green chile from Guadalupe's recipes that my mom loved during her days there. The tamales are the best I've ever eaten, a generous filling of red pork wrapped in a moist masa specked with visible bits of sweet yellow corn. The relleno is a purist's dream, dressed simply in a fluffy egg batter and stuffed with cheese. The enchilada is rolled and filled with onions and cheese and slathered in a smoky red chile that provides just the right sting. New Mexico has its own traditional taco that's easy to dismiss on a combo plate, but don't do that here. The meat in Chope's taco is sautéed with onions and perfectly seasoned, then stuffed inside a fried corn tortilla that also cradles shredded iceberg, diced toms, and thinly grated cheddar. The bar was added next door in 1949 and has become a popular stop for bikers cruising the scenic pecan orchards that fill the valleys along Highway 28 between Mesilla and El Paso, Texas. Despite the crowded dining rooms, the service is swift and efficient. (Waiters rarely write down orders, and the food comes fast.) For me, it's always worth the wait just to have a taste of home.

GOOD TO KNOW The line is always long, so try to hit it during non-peak hours. *16145 New Mexico Highway 28. (575) 233-3420; facebook.com/chopesbar.*

The Las Cruces Walk of Flame

Las Cruces, just forty miles southeast of Hatch down the Rio Grande, is Chile Central. So it makes perfect sense that the Las Cruces Convention and Visitors Center would create a Walk of Flame to guide visitors to the hottest chile spots around town. This trail is filled with surprising dishes, including a pecan and green chile sushi roll, green chile hummus, a green chile sundae, and green chile mashed potatoes. Yes, we put that stuff on everything. True fans might stick around for New Year's Eve, when the city drops a lighted chile instead of a crystal-covered ball. *lascrucescvb.org/explore/green-chile.*

Habaneros Fresh Mex in Las Cruces serves a respectable red (and green) as well as a popular chicken mole.

has perfected his take on the dish as the antidote to red chile weariness. A native of Zacatecas, Mexico, Chef Alfredo opened his little eatery in 2006 in an old adobe and is usually around to ensure that his customers leave full and happy. Of course, you can still order the Combo #1 here, and the red, green, and poblano sauces are all made fresh to satisfy the local need for the standards. But do yourself a favor and work through Felix's house specialties, which include spinach and artichoke enchiladas, arroz con pollo, and a few others you won't find on other New Mexican restaurant menus around town.

GOOD TO KNOW Give the breakfast options (served all day) a try. Again, you'll find items that don't appear frequently on menus in the area, including an avocado omelet and machaca (dried shredded beef) with eggs. *600 E. Amador Avenue. (575) 524–1829; habanerosfreshmexlcnm.com.*

Habaneros Fresh Mex

A little secret: New Mexicans get stuck in their ways and don't often branch out beyond their preferred Combo #1 at their favorite local restaurants. But if they did, they'd discover that a few restaurants have evolved beyond the red and green to deliver a range of other chile options. Habaneros does just that with its signature chicken mole. It's rich, smoky, and slightly sweet, just as the gods intended when the first cacao plant met its first dried red chile pod several centuries ago in a kitchen somewhere in Mexico. Habaneros' dish comes with a generous slathering of mole atop two juicy pieces of chicken and speckled with sesame seeds. The flour tortillas make the perfect mop-up tool for the remaining sauce. This modern mole is complex, hearty, and versatile, and chef-owner Alfredo Felix

Mesilla

La Posta de Mesilla

I was a traditional combination plate girl, while my dad always enthusiastically ordered the tostadas compuestas here. I hankered for those chiles rellenos, with a light batter covering a cheese-stuffed pod, taking up space next to a big goopy serving of Christmas-style enchiladas. But not long after my dad passed away in 2005, I decided to try the tostadas in his honor. And now I'm a convert. The *compuestas* (Spanish for "composed"), which La Posta claims were invented here, are fried tortilla shell cups holding red chile con carne and pinto beans, topped with grated cheddar, salsa, lettuce, and tomato (or Mexican slaw, if you want a little departure). Once you break through the lettuce, you'll find a treasure where the red chile soaks into the shell and the meat is tender and cheesy. Thanks, Dad.

A Word about Heat

When horticulturalist Fabián García began studying chiles in the early 1900s at the New Mexico College of Agriculture and Mechanic Arts in Las Cruces (now New Mexico State University), the goal was to create a pepper that had consistent flavor, size, and spiciness. You can learn more about the various varieties that have been developed here while touring NMSU's Chile Pepper Institute, which hosts a seasonal teaching garden as well as a gift shop for the dedicated chile fan. The most famous variety in the region is the Big Jim, known for its meatiness and dimensions that make the perfect chile relleno. But it can be spicy, and if you're not accustomed to a face-melting meal, you might think someone is pranking you. (A recent quote from my son: "I feel like I've been punched in the face—but in a good way.") But stick with it, and your tongue will adjust. A few tips: Order a glass of milk or a scoop of sour cream, as dairy helps soothe the burn. Others swear by a spoonful of honey. There's no shame in asking if the chile is hot today or requesting it on the side so that you can control the amounts. The rice and beans as well as the iceberg lettuce are also there to mitigate the burn. Most of the time, the chile is spicy but not overly so, but every once in a while you'll hit a place on a hot day. So wipe the sweat, keep eating, and know that what doesn't kill you only makes you happier.

The atmosphere is part of the package here too. The rambling rooms of this former stagecoach stop are filled with New Mexico art crammed into *nichos* (nooks embedded into thick adobe walls). While you dine, you'll hear the squawks of the parrots and cockatoos that serve as greeters (they'll talk to you too). (Read more in the margaritas chapter.)

GOOD TO KNOW The gift shops here are packed with cool local gifts, jewelry, and artwork, but they close pretty early, so go while you're waiting for your table. La Posta's sister restaurant is the Hacienda de Mesilla (haciendademesilla.com), located nearby on Avenida de Mesilla. Here the atmosphere is upscale and the menu leans into seafood and steak options (try the green chile crab bisque). *2410 Calle de San Albino. (575) 524-3524; laposta-de-mesilla.com.*

Ruidoso

Club Gas, Enchilada Night (Thursdays)

I walk cautiously along the side of the building. Gas pumps guard the front of this typical convenience store. Just to the right of it, a few stairs lead to a nondescript door. Weird that there are so many trucks, most bearing Texas license plates, parked where there doesn't seem to be a business. I open the door to reveal a low-lit room filled with folks talking, laughing, and watching a game on TV. It is almost like stepping into a speakeasy that hides its space and energy from the outside, or a New Mexican version of the TARDIS from *Dr. Who.* I find a table in the corner and hit the free chips and salsa station. It's Enchilada Night at Club Gas, a Thursday rite of passage. The plate of three homemade rolled enchiladas (red or green in beef, chicken, or cheese varieties) evokes a nostalgic sense that your mom has already made a big batch for anyone who

While You're Here: Ruidoso

Ruidoso is a fun little cowboy mountain town, packed with activities to keep you busy between meals. Following are a few highlights to check out:

RUIDOSO DOWNS RACE TRACK The Downs are a beautiful spot to watch the ponies and place a few wagers. Back in the '60s, folks flocked here to watch local celebrity jockey Willie Shoemaker. The Billy the Kid Casino is open year-round, but the racing season runs Mother's Day through June. *race ruidoso.com.*

INN OF THE MOUNTAIN GODS The Mescalero Apache Tribe owns this nicely appointed resort, and even nongamblers will appreciate the beauty and spirit that inhabits this 45,000-square-foot property. Various spaces here pay homage to the culture and art of the Mescaleros. The massive picture

The Inn of the Mountain Gods, owned by the Mescalero Apache Tribe, offers a golf course, a zipline, a casino, restaurants, a tap house, and other amenities.

windows in the lobby overlook a sparkling lake, framed by imposing mountains. Wendell's Steak and Seafood is the signature restaurant, but the Broken Arrow Tap House is a fine place to check out more than seventy beers on tap (many of them from New Mexico) as well as burgers and other gastropub fare. Activities here include ziplining, hunting, fishing, and skiing at nearby Ski Apache. *innofthemountaingods .com.*

SPENCER THEATER FOR THE PERFORMING ARTS The performing arts are alive and well in the Sacramento Mountains, and the 514-seat, $22 million theater is testament to that. Catch dance performances, concerts, plays, and other events at this top-notch facility, which also houses a collection of works by world-class glass artist Dale Chihuly. *spencertheater.com.*

FLYING J RANCH Did I mention that Ruidoso has deep western roots? This sprawling re-created Old West spread offers pony rides, cattle roping (dummies, not real cows), shopping, gunfights, cowboy fiddling and yodeling, and, best of all, an authentic chuckwagon dinner of brisket and other fixings—just like the old cowboy days. *flyingjranch.com.*

GALLERIES AND SHOPS Sudderth Drive is where you'll find the town's largest concentration of shops, offering everything from antiques and high-end boutiques to Christmas shops and galleries packed with works by local artists.

The Key

CHILI, THE TEXAS VERSION This is a stewy, tomato-based spicy dish that has beef and occasionally beans.

CHILE, THE PEPPER Don't write *chili* to refer to our beloved fruit or you will incur the wrath of all true New Mexicans.

CHILE, THE SAUCES This term is also applied to cooked or stewed versions of the pepper. For green chile, the fresh green pepper is roasted, peeled, chopped, and cooked with onions and garlic. It can be added to beef or chicken for a dish of its own. The red chile is a ripened green pepper that's been boiled down and strained from its peels and seeds. The resulting liquid is then cooked with salt, onions, garlic, and spices, per the cook's preferences. Both red and green chile can be used to top anything and everything.

Thursday nights are for enchiladas at Ruidoso's Club Gas, a gas station that operates a bar and small restaurant.

shows up. I look around and see an older gentleman holding court for a recent widow; others, in cowboy hats, are watching a small TV mounted near the bar. The waitress is busy but friendly. No one orders a fancy beer or a craft cocktail. It's about the atmosphere, the socializing, the chance to catch up on whose kids are in town for the summer and when they're going to get the fence fixed at the ranch. Here, the beer is served in a can and the plates are plain, but one bite and you're home.

GOOD TO KNOW This is a locals' secret, so don't worry that you can't find much about it among your usual online sources. You just have to trust me on this one. *1137 Mechem Drive. (575) 258-3211.*

6 Salt or No Salt?

Margaritas

Who knew that tequila paired with a squeeze of lime, a dash of orange liqueur, and a salty rim could result in such a fine way to watch a New Mexico sunset? But here I am, at a rooftop bar at a Santa Fe hotel, listening to the church bells fill the early evening air as the light casts orange and pink hues across the Sangre de Cristos.

While margaritas might've been invented in Mexico, New Mexico has certainly seized upon the basic recipe and shaken it up a bit—literally. I like to believe that part of the reason they're so good here is because of the atmosphere—the sipping often occurs in beautiful spaces, surrounded by adobe walls or overlooking desert views.

The other reason our margaritas transcend is our tendency to liven up the classics with a bit of spice. We'll blend the lime with just a bite of jalapeño or use a dash of red chile powder on the rim with the salt, inducing the perfect lip burn. For an edge of smokiness, you might find yourself sipping a margarita made with mezcal. Or take a virtual trip to the desert by imbibing a marg made with the earthy fruit of the prickly pear. In short, our mixologists take the beverage seriously here, so if you always request the house margarita, you're cheating yourself out of some creative and flavorful sips.

While you can find this beverage just about everywhere in the state, Santa Fe is the reigning HQ for the limey drink. If you faithfully follow the city's Margarita Trail (see page 65), you will stay busy awhile and rarely be disappointed. The drinkeries at the southern end of the state will treat you right too, so don't be shy about exploring those menus.

This chapter is by no means a comprehensive guide but is rather a curated selection of options that offer superior atmosphere, talented bartenders, or just a great place to duck in, take off your hat, and cool off for a spell. ¡Salúd!

The art of combining lime, salt, and tequila achieves great heights in New Mexico.

Taos

TOP PICK

Adobe Bar and Doc Martin's, Taos Inn

A chupacabra, the Buddha, and a horny toad walked into the Adobe Bar in Taos. Well, it might not have quite gone down that way, but these three characters do meet on this extensive, nongimmicky margarita menu that is worthy of the town in which they are served. El Chupacabra is named for

Doc Martin's puts a fresh twist on classic margaritas at the Taos Inn.

While You're Here: Taos

TAOS PLAZA New Mexico towns tend to centralize around a plaza, thanks to Spanish influences in force in the 1600s and 1700s, when the area was being colonized for the king of Spain. Taos is no different, and these days the plaza still serves as a gathering place. During summer, folks assemble at the gazebo to listen to live music and to dance. Year-round the shops, galleries, and eateries make for a fun day of exploration. *taos.org.*

THE ARTS Taos is the epicenter of New Mexico's art scene, thanks to several waves of artists who infiltrated this colorful community. These days, there is no shortage of art, whether it's seen in the town's outdoor sculptures or inside its museums and galleries. Highlights include the Harwood Museum of Art (*575-758-9826; harwoodmuseum.org*), the Taos Art Museum at Fechin House (*575-758-2690; taosartmuseum.org*), and the Millicent Rogers Museum (*575-758-2462; millicentrogers.org*).

THE GORGE AT RIO GRANDE DEL NORTE NATIONAL MONUMENT Talk about a photo op. The Gorge, carved eight hundred feet down by the Rio Grande, creates a scenic stopover and also a haven for recreation. You can stay up top and just enjoy the view, or you can raft, hike, bike, and camp down below at this national monument, a swath of 244,555 acres that was preserved by a presidential proclamation in 2013. *blm.gov/visit/rgdnnm.*

TAOS PUEBLO No matter how many times I've visited Taos Pueblo, I still am awestruck by its beauty and the warmth of the people who live here. Yes, despite its age (established roughly around one thousand years ago) and its mudded, rustic exterior, the pueblo is still a residence, so visitors must be mindful. You can wander on your own, but the tours provide a much deeper look at the history of the pueblo and a culture that runs as deep today as it did hundreds of years ago. *taospueblo.com.*

the mythical beast from Mexico, and the namesake drink captures his feisty spirit with the use of green pepper–infused tequila with a salt-and-pepper rim. The Horny Toad is all about the Hornitos Añejo tequila, while the Cowboy Buddha, one of the most popular options, is simple but leans on quality ingredients (just Patron Silver, Cointreau, and fresh-squeezed lime juice). Take all that in while you enjoy the Taos Inn's easygoing atmosphere, a spot where live music keeps toes tapping nearly every evening and often late into the night. (Read more in the "Green and Red" chapter.)

GOOD TO KNOW If you're not a local, you should plan to enjoy the music and margaritas and then stay overnight in one of the inn's forty-five charming guest rooms, many of which include kiva fireplaces. *125 Paseo del Pueblo Norte. (575) 425–0169; taosinn.com.*

Santa Fe

Anasazi Bar and Lounge, Rosewood Inn of the Anasazi

This is where we go when we want to go "full Santa Fe." The hosts dress in western attire, the decor is upscale rustic Southwest, and the staff is exceedingly gracious and welcoming. Tourists tend to collect here, so

EARTHSHIPS Along with a deep and evolving arts community, a thriving farm-to-table food scene, and a peacenik vibe throughout, Taos's hippie roots have also spawned some interesting architectural offshoots. Earthships, a name that evokes a distinctive cosmic vibe, are this community's answer to sustainable housing and have been attracting attention ever since New Mexico architect Michael Reynolds designed the first ones in the 1970s. These alternative-energy dwellings, built with upcycled and natural materials, are innovative and artistic. They not only combat climate change but also offer off-the-grid, affordable housing options in the desert. Visitors can tour some of Taos's Earthships, located northwest of town. Some are available for nightly and short-term rental. The visitor center is open weekdays, and self-guided tours are available. *earthshipglobal.com.*

SAN FRANCISCO DE ASIS CHURCH, RANCHOS DE TAOS It's been sketched, photographed, and painted by such artistic luminaries as Georgia O'Keeffe, Ansel Adams, and R. C. Gorman. Over more than two hundred years, it's been visited by thousands of people. Its massive buttresses, twin bell towers, and picturesque adobe walls, contrasted against aqua New Mexico skies, make it irresistibly photogenic. Folks come together every year to re-mud and preserve the old structure (volunteers are welcome). While you're there, be sure to stop at the visitor center to watch a short documentary film and see *The Shadow of the Cross*, a painting of Jesus that, in the dark, seems to glow with images of a boat and a cross that are not visible in the light. Best $3 you'll ever spend.

TAOS SKI VALLEY Yes, it's first and foremost a world-class ski resort, offering more than 3,100 vertical feet of schussable terrain. But in the summer, you'll also find scenic chairlift rides that lead to hiking and picnicking spots, mountain bike trails and rentals, and other outdoor activities. *skitaos.com.*

Social hour at the Anasazi Bar and Lounge in Santa Fe means that mixologists find fresh ways to spice up the standard margarita.

the people-watching is prime: You'll see folks who've just hit up the high-end plaza shops for fancy gator cowboy boots and oversize turquoise jewelry. The margaritas and cocktails rise to the level of everything else here, and the bartenders will guide you should you need advice. (There's also a dedicated tequila-tasting table, if that's any indication.)

GOOD TO KNOW The official dress code here is "smart casual," and social hour at the bar is 3–5:30 p.m. nightly. *113 Washington Avenue. (505) 988-3030; rosewoodhotels.com.*

El Callejón Taqueria and Grill

Some of us prefer our margaritas with a side of street tacos, and thankfully there's a place for us. Tucked into a side street off the plaza, this pretty little hole in the wall is a great place to rejuvenate while you chow

down on carne asada tacos that pair just right with an icy house margarita. The bar is the focal point here, and the rustic furniture and blown-glass barware give it a distinct Oaxacan vibe.

GOOD TO KNOW The house-made chips and salsa here are to die for, but they cost extra (about $5). *208 Galisteo Street. (505) 983-8378; elcallejonsantafe.com.*

Cowgirl Santa Fe

Santa Fe's western heart beats loudly here. You'll find local musicians, well-crafted barbecue and burgers, a friendly bar, and an atmosphere of conviviality. That's why, after a long day of tramping through the desert, my sister and I ended up there to meet some friends on a warm summer evening. Unfortunately, my sister had just landed on her backside atop a prickly pear cactus, so after we spent a few minutes pulling spines out of her britches, we opted for the prickly pear margarita to soothe both of our pains and to celebrate desert life with our friends. The house marg here is refreshing, not too sweet and with just enough agave spirit to ease a smile across your face. I can recommend every margarita they serve (and there's a frozen option here too), but when I'm celebrating, I go right to the Cadillac, a happy combo of *añejo* (aged) tequila, a squeeze of both orange and lime, and a red chile–salt rim. (Read more in the "Green Chile Cheeseburger" chapter.)

GOOD TO KNOW Check out live music on weekends. *319 S. Guadalupe Street. (505) 982-2565; cowgirlsantafe.com.*

Coyote Cantina, Coyote Café

All the pretty people gather on the compact rooftop bar just upstairs from Coyote Café, founded in 1987 by chef Mark Miller, a pioneer of haute southwestern cuisine. While watching a parade of well-heeled tourists and locals meandering the plaza, you can enjoy the Norteño, a spicy concoction made with green chile–infused tequila. You'll eat too many of the perfectly salted and crispy chips and salsa, but leave room for the ceviche or green enchiladas.

GOOD TO KNOW The Coyote Café is one of Santa Fe's trendiest eateries, so the menu and margaritas are on the pricier side. But the cantina serves casual, well-above-average cuisine made from locally sourced ingredients. *132 W. Water Street. (505) 983–1615; coyotecafe.com.*

El Farol

Did I mention that atmosphere was half the recipe for New Mexico's best margaritas? That's especially true in this legendary Santa Fe hideaway, where you can enjoy your margs and Spanish tapas with a side of hard-stomping, skirt-flipping flamenco. The restaurant also features live music Tuesday through Saturday. Locals favor small bites and beverages at the cozy bar, where you can order up the El Farol Margarita, the perfect pairing to Spanish guitar on select nights. The people-watching from the Canyon Road–facing narrow bar is superb. It's a prime spot to enjoy a margarita and ponder the fact that this spot has helped slake the thirst of weary Santa Fe patrons since its inception in the 1830s. (Read more in the "Green Chile Cheeseburger" chapter.)

GOOD TO KNOW The flamenco performances are designed as a dinner and a show; reservations are required and there is a $30 cover charge in addition to your meal. *808 Canyon Road. (505) 983–9912; elfarol-santafe.com.*

TOP PICK

La Fiesta Lounge and the Bell Tower Bar, La Fonda

The bars at La Fonda are where everyone comes together. Meeting someone to talk about New Mexico politics? Try La Fiesta

Lounge. Ready to take a walking tour of Santa Fe? Done with a hard day of shopping on the plaza? Wrapping up a day on the Ski Santa Fe slopes? The Bell Tower awaits. Any of these activities might begin or conclude with one of the hotel's famously delicious and limey margaritas. La Fiesta is at the center of the lobby and offers a limited menu; it's a centralized place to meet for a well-prepared margarita and a light meal. There's music on most evenings on the small stage, and locals like to cut a rug here too. Or head upstairs to the Bell Tower Bar, where you can take in expansive views of Santa Fe as you sip. I've worked my way through most of the tequila-based beverages here, and while I'm hard-pressed to pick a favorite, the Tower Sunset, with its Espolón Blanco and hint of pomegranate, goes down as smoothly as the New Mexico sun fades on the western horizon. (Read more in the breakfast chapter.)

GOOD TO KNOW Bring your cowboy hat and sunglasses if you're going to sit at the

Folks meet at La Fonda's Bell Tower Bar and La Fiesta Lounge for sunset watching, socializing, and margarita sipping.

A creative cocktail menu pairs with a lowrider theme at the Low 'N Slow at Santa Fe's Hotel Chimayó.

Records. Mixologists run the bar here, concocting custom cocktails like the popular Zephyr, a complex beverage made with a smoky mezcal and a flavorful vermouth and then shaken together with a dose of blood orange juice.

GOOD TO KNOW During the warmer months, the hotel offers tours in a 1964 Chevy Impala lowrider (for hotel guests only as of press time, but plans to open them to others are in the works). *125 Washington Avenue. (505) 988–4900; hotel chimayo.com.*

Maria's New Mexican Kitchen

This 1950s classic locals' Mexican eatery offers a seven-page margarita list, but I love the house margarita and, truthfully, can usually handle only one—this place doesn't skimp on its pours. Most of the variations on the list are made with different tequilas and agave-based liquors (which can't be called tequila unless they're made in a

Bell Tower—it's only partially covered, and the sun can be intense, especially during the height of summer. *100 E. San Francisco Street. (505) 982–5511; lafondasantafe.com.*

Low 'N Slow Lowrider Bar, Hotel Chimayó de Santa Fe

The lowrider culture is alive and well in northern New Mexico, and if you're lucky, you might see examples of these airbrushed beauties cruising the Santa Fe Plaza on a warm summer night. The culture is deeply celebrated at the Low 'N Slow Lowrider Bar, where the decor honors the fuzzy dice, slick paint jobs, custom rims, and other chromed elements of the lowrider car. Grab a seat behind the chain steering wheel tables or poke around on the vintage jukebox, which offers an eclectic mix curated by local music store Lost Padre

The massive margarita menu at Maria's New Mexican Kitchen offers an homage to Zozobra and other local notables.

Santa Fe Margarita Trail

We all like goals, right? Pick up a paper booklet ($3) or download the Santa Fe Margarita Trail app ($2.99) and work your way through a list of forty-five margaritas, scattered among the bars and restaurants in and around the City Different. It would be like choosing a favorite child to name the best one, but I prefer the Nooner at Casa Sena near the plaza, which comes with entertainment provided by the restaurant's singing servers. The GOAT Cabrito at Harry's Roadhouse (pictured) is shaken, not stirred, and comes with the shaker on the side to ensure you get every last drop. (And it strains out the ice.) Present your app or booklet to get stamped (no more than two per day) and receive

Take a tour of Santa Fe's restaurants and bars through its Margarita Trail.

$1 off. Once you get five stamps, you can cash in for a Margarita Trail T-shirt. Complete the trail and you're eligible for a VIP Margarita Package, which is customized to your experiences and preferences.

specific region in Mexico), including a few made in New Mexico. La Margarita de Paradiso, which sells for $48, is made with aged El Tesoro agave liquor and hundredth-anniversary Cuvee Centenaire Grand Marnier. Former owner Al Lucero literally wrote the book on margaritas, *The Great Margarita Book* (so he could say he wrote the book on margaritas), and the margarita list here offers homages to longtime employees and local celebrities, including actor-director Robert Redford and New Mexico–born jockey Mike Smith, who rode Zenyatta, a star racehorse that won nineteen consecutive races out of twenty. There's also a wide range of fruity blended margaritas for my sister, who prefers hers to be slushy, as well as a selection made with infused tequilas (like jalapeño and chocolate). There are even some made with other

boozes, in case anyone's allergic to tequila (we've all been there). During Zozobra season, when Santa Feans burn a giant effigy of Old Man Gloom in September, Maria's offers a special flaming version in a collectible glass.

GOOD TO KNOW Maria's also features an extensive wine list. *555 W. Cordova Road. (505) 983–7929; marias-santafe.com.*

La Reina, El Rey Court

This renovated motor court dating to 1936, during the Route 66 heyday, reopened in 2018 with one of Santa Fe's hippest watering holes. The white adobe walls of the bar evoke a minimalist vibe, but that doesn't mean the drinks are light on flavor or craft. The King's Margarita is a good start, but I often gravitate away from the traditional to the Negroni Rubia, a twist on the classic negroni made with mezcal. The extensive agave spirits menu, offering a range of tequilas, mezcals, and sotols (another plant-based booze imported from Mexico), will make you want to linger. In the summer, the pool opens to nonguests who join the swim club, lending a Palm Springs vibe to the scene. **GOOD TO KNOW** Catch live music here. *1862 Cerrillos Road. (505) 982–1931; elrey court.com.*

Tomasita's

"I don't like the margaritas with the ice cubes in them," my sister defiantly told me one fine summer day as I ordered a fancy on-the-rocks version at a chichi Santa Fe bar. We were there to meet a friend whose family has lived in Santa Fe for generations. I was mortified. "How pedestrian," I thought, and I made a joke at my sister's expense about how some people just don't understand the highbrow craft of margaritas. But my friend piped up that she knew someone who shared this view, adding that there's a strong contingent of folks who love the old-school, Slurpee-style blended margaritas and can shamelessly order them at Tomasita's. My mortification turned to curiosity, especially when she mentioned that the restaurant offers a twist on the classic known as the Swirl, a beautiful melding of a blended margarita and sangria. It's on the sweet side, so it goes down quickly. But don't be fooled into thinking you can drink them all day and not feel it. With the help of the strolling mariachi performers on Tuesday nights, I'll proudly proclaim that I'm a blended margarita convert—at least at Tomasita's. **GOOD TO KNOW** Tomasita's also has an Albuquerque location at 4949 Pan American Freeway NE. *500 S. Guadalupe Street. (505) 983–5721; tomasitas.com.*

Albuquerque

El Pinto Restaurant and Cantina

With more than 150 brands of tequila and mezcal filling the shelves here, the drink decisions can be mind-boggling. But you can be sure that your margarita will be made with special attention to the ingredients, right down to the house-made simple syrup and fresh-squeezed citrus. This legendary destination restaurant is on a rambling North Valley property owned and operated by twin brothers Jim and John Thomas, who also produce nationally distributed El Pinto salsas (available at grocery stores) as well as fine New Mexican food. This place is massive—it can seat more than two hundred diners—and in the summer, the chile ristra– and plant-covered patio is the best place to chow down on chips and salsa with a margarita. (Pick one made with one the El Pinto's premium tequilas, and you won't be sorry.) You can hear live music most days, and in the past, they've offered yoga sessions on Sundays during the summer.

GOOD TO KNOW El Pinto's Hen Hotel provides fresh eggs for the restaurant through its laying hen program, which is "Animal Welfare Approved" by A Greener World, an independent, nonprofit farm certification program. *10500 Fourth Street NW. (505) 898–1771; elpinto.com.*

High Noon Restaurant and Saloon

From the outside, this appears to be a rustic Old Town adobe dating back two hundred years (which it is), but enter through the low-hanging, narrow doorway, and you'll find a rambling hacienda-style restaurant, with nichos filled with saints, a cozy kiva fireplace, and a busy but comfortable bar that wraps through the center of it all. While I typically recommend a close menu-reading and choosing one of the specialties, the house margarita is the way to go here (especially when it's happy hour, 3–6 p.m. on weekdays). It's made with fresh-squeezed lime, tequila, and simple syrup, and is frothy and refreshing. The daily special is almost always an interesting combination of flavors, such as hibiscus and mint. I favor the Down the Hatch, a smooth beverage made with red chile–infused simple syrup, Corazon Silver, fresh lime, and a piñon salt rim. (Read more in the "Green and Red" chapter.)

GOOD TO KNOW The carved saints tucked into the nichos are an Instagrammer's dream. *425 San Felipe Street NW. (505) 765–1455; highnoonrestaurant.com.*

The Award-Winner Margarita is the go-to at Double Eagle's elegant Imperial Bar in Mesilla.

Las Cruces

Imperial Bar, Double Eagle, Mesilla

This is one of the most beautiful bars in all of southern New Mexico, and it serves some pretty good drinks too. Perch yourself in front of this hand-carved, gold-leafed beauty, under the French chandeliers, and order the Award-Winner Margarita, made from the same recipe for thirty years. My second pick: the Cucumber-n-Chile (made with roasted jalapeño–infused silver tequila) paired with the green chile wontons from the bar menu. (Read more in the green chile cheeseburger chapter.)

GOOD TO KNOW Sunday brunch at the Double Eagle is legendary and includes a complimentary glass of champagne and corn tortillas made on the spot (which you

High Noon Restaurant and Saloon's margarita menu offers intriguing specials, including concoctions with hibiscus, mint, and other innovative ingredients.

also can take home by the dozen).
2355 Calle de Guadalupe. (575) 523–6700;
doubleeagleonline.com.

La Posta de Mesilla, Mesilla

There's nothing better on a hot southern
New Mexico day than ducking into a cool
old adobe for an authentic, well-crafted
margarita. And La Posta delivers. This
locals' and tourists' favorite is tucked inside
an 1840s building that was formerly a stagecoach stop on the Butterfield Trail, which
carried passengers and mail from Memphis
and St. Louis to San Francisco. The place
was a hotel for a stretch and became the
restaurant we know and love in 1939. Enter
through the heavy wooden doors to the
lobby, where a collection of noisy parrots
and cockatoos greet as you wait for a table.
Or you can head directly to the small bar,
where you can do what smart diners do and
pair a margarita with La Posta's famed
chiles rellenos or tostadas compuestos.
Popular options include the Chile Rita,
which combines Hornitos Reposado with a
locally made concoction known as Besito
Caliente, a mix of berries and habanero.
The Mesilla Valley Cucumber Jalapeño version is refreshing and spicy, fusing mud-
dled cukes with jalapeños; local honey
binds local pecans and green chile–flavored
salt to the rim. (Read more in the "Green
and Red" chapter.)

GOOD TO KNOW Breakfast is served here
on weekends and should be ordered with a
famous La Posta Bloody Maria, made with
tequila. *2410 Calle de San Albino. (575) 524–
3524; laposta-de-mesilla.com.*

La Posta in Mesilla offers an extensive
tequila menu and a range of creative
margarita options.

Roswell

Antigua Cocina Mexicana

Just when you think New Mexico's small
towns hold few culinary surprises, along
comes Antigua in Roswell. Artfully deco-
rated like an upscale Mexico City eatery,
this hip spot serves elevated versions of traditional Mexican food. With that, of course,
comes elevated margaritas made from a
selection of well-curated tequilas. The classic Antigua Margarita is made with
reposado ("rested" or aged) tequila and is a
fine accompaniment to the popular queso
fundido appetizer or flame-cooked Black

Antigua Cocina Mexicana in Roswell concocts creative cocktails with a Mexico City vibe.

The frosty refresher served at Peppers Grill and Bar in Roswell comes in a saguaro stem glass.

Angus rib eye fajitas. Overall, the entire experience might make you forget you're in Roswell, which is better known for its UFO history (the alleged 1947 alien ship crash site) and related attractions.

GOOD TO KNOW You can make a meal out of Antigua Cocina's happy hour, which features $4 house margaritas and half-price appetizers, such as rib eye nachos and shrimp cocktail made with massive shrimps and house-made sauce. Happy hour is 2 to 6 p.m. Monday through Saturday. *3601 N. Main Street. (575) 208-0991; antiguacm.com.*

Peppers Grill and Bar

I love a margarita served in a glass with a saguaro stem. I'll even occasionally over-look a bland sweet-and-sour mix in the name of good glassware. Thankfully, I don't have to sacrifice anything here. These margaritas are made fresh and served in those fancy glasses. The bonus? On Margarita Mondays, you can get them for $3 each (including the frozen one, which my sister prefers and I mercilessly make fun of her for). The Famous Peppers Margarita is the go-to, but the restaurant does delicious raspberry and mango versions too.

GOOD TO KNOW During Peppers gener-ous happy hour, which runs 4:30–7:30 p.m. nightly, house margaritas are $4 (and $3 on Margarita Mondays). *500 N. Main St. (575) 623-1700; peppers-grill.com.*

7 Foam on the Range
Craft Beer

Cheers to New Mexico's craft beer industry! With more than eighty-five breweries in the state, New Mexico is ranked tenth in the nation for its ratio of breweries to drinking-age adults, according to the Boulder, Colorado–based Brewers Association.

I, for one, am grateful for this movement—for multiple reasons that go beyond the fact that I like beer. Not only is the craft a boon to the state's economy; it also reflects a lean toward quality and creativity. The locally made beer distributed in New Mexico and beyond is like an advertisement for our state. Case in point: Much of the bottle and can art, as well as the names of the brews, reflects state pride, capturing everything from Zias to our epic mountain-scapes. Secondly, craft breweries have become social spaces that reflect a New Mexico aesthetic, with nods toward Native American, Spanish, Mexican, and Anglo influences.

New Mexico is home to more than eighty-five craft breweries serving an array of award-winning brews.

Winning Brews

New Mexican beers are winners, proof of which can be found in the sheer number of medals that adorn our bottles and taps. The Great American Beer Festival in Denver annually attracts thousands of beer devotees to discover new favorites, and several New Mexico–made beers have been honored over the years at this prestigious national competition. I use the breweries that earned accolades in 2017, 2018, and 2019 as an initial measuring stick to pare down the state's ever-growing list of breweries.

The foodie culture pairs well too, going hand in hand with our creative bevvies. Thirdly, a thriving microbrew scene reflects our passions: We are mountain bikers, skiers, hikers, and yoga practitioners, and there's nothing better than enjoying a hard-earned brew after a day beneath those New Mexico bluebird skies. Lastly, and most notably, New Mexico beers are good, whether they're coming out of the big tanks in Albuquerque or the small ones in places like Truth or Consequences.

We must give some credit to Albuquerque for taking the trend and running with it. Duke City is where our state's youth culture tends to roost, and this generation's love of hops has provided major fuel that's fed the rest of the state. At current count, Albuquerque is home to more than thirty microbreweries and taprooms. Santa Fe keeps the bar high too, presenting a hoppy face to the droves of tourists who flock there, reminding them through our brews that we know what we're doing here in New Mexico. Las Cruces is by no means tapping out, filling the mugs of college students, retirees, and everyone in between.

The craft brew industry also sources locally. Several of our breweries use a subvariety of hops called *neomexicanus*. Native to New Mexico, it thrives in the sunshine and high mountain climate here. And the spent hops often goes back to local farmers as feed for livestock.

New Mexico craft beer is not just a beverage; it's an experience that is reflective of this place of deep culture and wide-open spaces. So let's go brewery hopping. Allow this guide to serve as a sampling, or a flight if you will, of the state's breweries, all of which stand out for a multitude of reasons. For more, check out the New Mexico Brewers Guild map at nmbeer.org.

Cheers to the well-crafted IPAs and live performances served at Second Street Brewery in Santa Fe.

Santa Fe

Rowley Farmhouse Ales

This small but mighty brewery cleaned up at the 2019 Great American Beer Festival, nabbing the Small Brewpub and Small Brewpub Brewer of the Year honors, as well as a few nods for its unique brews. The owners and brewers know their stuff and aren't afraid to go beyond the basic IPA. They offer a variety of fruited sours and an English barley wine. The food game stands out too: This is beyond a doubt the best place to enjoy chicken and waffles in this swath of the non-South. (The chicken biscuit sandwich is a very close second.)

GREAT AMERICAN BEER FEST WINNERS
Meier (Gold, 2019, German-style sour ale); Cote d'Or, Double Cerise (Bronze, 2019, mixed-culture brett beer); Agent Orange,

Apple Brandy Barrel (Silver, 2019, wood- and barrel-aged sour beer); Germophile (Silver, 2018, Berliner-style weisse). *1405 Maclovia Street. (505) 428–0719; rowley farmhouse.com.*

Second Street Brewery

What pairs best with Cajun tater tots? Perhaps an Agua Fria Pilsner. Or a Sloppy Sloth IPA. Oh, who are we kidding? All beers go with tots—and vice versa. And if good beer with a neighborly vibe is what you're after, this place is like a comfy living room, whether you settle in among the wood-paneled walls at the original location on Second Street or the more modern spot with picture windows overlooking the Railyard near the Santa Fe Depot. The Rufina Taproom is the best place to recover from an outing to nearby Meow Wolf's House of Eternal Return, an interactive art installation that defies explanation. Among Second Street's three locations, you'll find live music, beer-centric celebrations, arts and crafts bazaars, and other accompaniments to these fine brews. The menus are slightly different at each location; the tater tots are only available at Rufina.

GREAT AMERICAN BEER FEST WINNERS
Rod's Steam Bitter (Bronze, 2017, American-style amber lager). *1607 Paseo de Peralta; (505) 989–3278. 1814 Second Street; (505) 982–3030. 2920 Rufina Street. (505) 954–1068. secondstreetbrewery.com.*

Tumbleroot Brewery and Distillery

With its superb craft brews, house-made spirits, kids' play area, expansive seating, and stage showcasing local performers, Tumbleroot is a popular and lively place to hang out any time of year. But my favorite time to be there is on a warm summer Santa Fe afternoon, with a Honey Hibiscus Wheat and soft pretzel in hand, sitting on the outdoor benches in the shade of the big ol' trees on the open-air patio, enjoying the

New Mexico vibe. The kitchen serves good food, or you can belly up to the food trucks that often park outside. Tip: Don't overlook Tumbleroot's spirits, which are included on the inventive cocktail menu. And do yourself a favor and pick up a bottle of Tumbleroot Botanical Gin or Tumbleroot Farmhouse Whisky at a regional liquor store. (Read more about Tumbleroot in the wine and spirits chapter.)

GREAT AMERICAN BEER FEST WINNER Double Brown Ale (Bronze, 2019, other strong beer). *2791 Agua Fria Street. (505) 780–5730; tumblerootbreweryand distillery.com.*

Bernalillo

Bosque Brewing Company

This brewery, with its strong roster of more than a dozen beers and a thriving package business, has been quietly blossoming since it opened its doors in 2012. It strives to be a community hangout, opening a sprawling operation in north Albuquerque to join its Nob Hill installment and operating multiple locations in Las Cruces. It consistently wins awards for its Pistol Pete's 1888 Ale, a nod to the pistol-packing mascot of New Mexico State University, where Bosque has earned a loyal following. The beers here are superb on tap and come in eight varieties in cans (including the aforementioned Pistol Pete's), which you can conveniently grab in area grocery stores for the home fridge. My pick here is Elephants on Parade, a tart wheat ale that always hits the spot.

GREAT AMERICAN BEER FEST WINNERS Pistol Pete's 1888 Ale (Bronze, 2018, golden or blonde ale). *Bosque North Brewery and Taproom: 834 U.S. Highway 550, Bernalillo; (505) 361–1876. Nob Hill Public House: 106 Girard Boulevard SE, Suite B; (505) 508–5967. Santa Fe Market Station Public House: 500 Market Street, Suite 110A; (505) 557–6672.*

Las Cruces: 901 E. University Avenue; (575) 888–4110; 2102 Telshor Court; (575) 556–9128. bosquebrewing.com.

Rio Rancho

Turtle Mountain Brewing Company

Pizza and beer is about the best pairing you could ever "hop for," and this is one of the best places in New Mexico to experience it. The Truchas—a pie made with marinara, artichoke hearts, roasted red peppers, and lightly toasted pine nuts—makes a heavenly mouthful when paired with the Wooden Teeth American Lager made with German hops. Established in 1999, ahead of the first craft brew wave, this brewery has developed into a homey neighborhood hangout.

GREAT AMERICAN BEER FEST WINNERS Wooden Teeth (Gold, 2018, international-style pilsner). *905 36th Place SE. (505) 994–9497; turtlemountainbrewing.com.*

Albuquerque

Boxing Bear Brewing Company

These beers pop up on taps throughout New Mexico, adding fresh options to fill your frosty glass no matter where you are in the state. There's a taproom downtown, but I favor the brewery perched right on the Rio Grande. My pour of choice is the Featherweight Session IPA, but I'm also drawn to the Chocolate Milk Stout, a former Great American Beer Fest multimedalist, which you can now pick up by the four-pack.

GREAT AMERICAN BEER FEST WINNER Featherweight Session IPA (Bronze, 2017, India pale ale). *10200 Corrales Road NW; (505) 897–2327. 1710 Central Avenue SW; (505) 897–2327. Bridges on Tramway Taproom: 12501 Candelaria Road NE; (505) 639–4983. boxingbearbrewing.com.*

La Cumbre Brewing Company

The well-crafted taproom in Northeast Albuquerque (plus another on the West Side) has a strong New Mexico vibe, with license plate lamps and southwestern-themed fantasy artwork on the walls. The brewery distributes to regional stores and bars, and its chunky and colorful can art is among my faves. Top beer? Elevated IPA is always a go-to, and Project Dank is well rated and worth sampling. Hang out for food trucks, yoga, and other events.

GREAT AMERICAN BEER FEST WINNER Acclimated APA (Silver, 2019, American-style pale ale); Malpais Stout (Silver, 2018, export stout). *3313 Girard NE; (505) 872–0225. 5600 Coors Boulevard NW; (505) 916–0787. lacumbrebrewing.com.*

TOP PICK

Marble Brewery

Founded in 2008, this early adopter brewery has developed a loyal following and reputation as one of the Albuquerque beer kings. (It ranked second in the number of barrels produced in the state in 2018.) The taprooms—downtown, Northeast Heights, and West Side—are low-key, and the beers are ubiquitous in New Mexico grocery and liquor stores. My go-to is the Marble Desert Fog, a hazy IPA that has a designated spot in our beverage fridge. Aficionados should take the free (and fun) tours, offered Saturdays at 2 p.m. at the downtown location and the first Sunday of the month at 3 p.m. in Northeast Heights (birthplace of the popular Cholo Stout). There are no kitchens, but food trucks keep imbibers fed.

GREAT AMERICAN BEER FEST WINNER Cholo Stout (Gold, 2017, American-style stout); Pilsner (Bronze, 2017, Kellerbier or Zwickelbier). *Downtown: 111 Marble Avenue NW; (505) 243–2739. Westside: 5740 Night Whisper Road NW; (505) 508–4368.*

Northeast Heights: 9904 Montgomery Boulevard NE; (505) 323–4030. marblebrewery.com.

Nexus Restaurant, Taproom, Smokehouse

Smoked meats pair well with beers, and this dark-walled, modern-style brewery does both well. Owner Ken Carson was inspired by a *Star Trek* reference—when Picard and Kirk experience the Nexus, a dimension in which desires become reality. We don't have to go deep into science fiction to appreciate the effects of this Nexus, where you can sip the lovely Honey Chamomile Wheat while noshing on a southern-fried chicken sandwich or the New Mexico Nachos, which are smothered in red or green chile and beefed up with a smoked ham hock. A second location, the Nexus Blue Smokehouse, leans even more into the smoked meats—the pulled pork sandwich and brisket make it worth hitting up both places.

GREAT AMERICAN BEER FEST WINNER Imperial Cream Ale (Gold, 2017, other strong beer). *4730 Pan American Freeway NE, Suite D; (505) 242–4100. Smokehouse: 1511 Broadway Blvd. NE; (505) 445–1545. nexusbrewery.com.*

Starr Brothers Brewing Company

The atmosphere is lively and noisy here, with multiple screens showing games and plenty of families enjoying an evening out. But don't think this hot spot doesn't take the beer or the food seriously. This popular hangout brews one of my favorite pilsners, the Starrphire, and serves a mean green chile cheeseburger topped with a green chile aioli. (Why isn't that a thing everywhere?) Head brewer Rob Whitlock offers on-demand tours of the operation, so if beer-making is your thing, Rob's your man.

GREAT AMERICAN BEER FEST WINNER Lampshade Porter (Bronze, 2018, other strong beer). *5700 San Antonio Drive NE. (505) 492–2752; starrbrothersbrewing.com.*

Toltec Brewing

The menu is as critically tended to here as the taps, as is noted by the 2018 James Beard Award–winning Royale, a cremini mushroom and beef–blended burger. The hearty burger is topped with a fried egg, bacon, and green chile and then wrapped in a brioche bun. Wash that down with the Sacred ALTar, a German-style altbier amber, or the Lupulin Guardian IPA. The tacos are worth the trip too.

GREAT AMERICAN BEER FEST WINNER Shaman Stout (Bronze, 2019, oatmeal stout). *10250 Cottonwood Park NW. (505) 890–1455; toltecbrewing.com.*

Moriarty

Sierra Blanca Brewing Company

Established in 1996 in Carrizozo, this brewery later moved to Moriarty east of Albuquerque. At this half-acre beer garden, folks can sip craft brews, play cornhole on the lawn, listen to live music, grab sustenance off a food truck, and stretch out a bit. The beers are great year-round, but the award-winning Cherry Wheat is a superb summer sipper. The brewery also makes a pretty tasty Green Chile Cerveza, a worthy toast during our state's favorite harvest season. The Rio Grande Grill and Taproom, located in Ruidoso, serves the same great brews plus a deep menu, featuring St. Louis–style ribs and an extensive array of pasta dishes.

GREAT AMERICAN BEER FEST WINNER Cherry Wheat (Silver, 2019; Bronze, 2018; Gold, 2017; fruit wheat beer). *1016 Industrial Road; (505) 832–2337. Ruidoso Taproom: 441 Mechem Drive; (575) 808–8456. sierrablancabrewery.com.*

DON'T OVERLOOK THESE GUYS

New Mexico's craft beer industry isn't governed by awards alone. Some have been quietly brewing great beers for many years, relying either on past awards or a loyal customer base. Some are also new on the scene, while others are just great places to hang out, offering inviting spaces, humble hospitality, scenic surroundings, and, in some instances, good eats to go with those brews.

Taos

Taos Mesa Brewing

This brewery is more than just a place to grab a brewski—it's a Taos institution. The Mothership, as it is called, sits just a stone's throw from the Gorge Bridge. It suffered damage during a devastating fire in July 2020 but should be back in 2021, beckoning beer lovers as well as music fans to its cavernous converted airplane hangar. The brews are still in production and represent the IPA realm admirably; the ciders have a strong following here as well. But this is a town that loves music, and the stages out here are a destination unto themselves. Festivals and big-name musicians are de rigueur here, especially in the spring and summer months, when we can all sit outside and enjoy the high-elevation cooldown. In town, the Taos Tap Room has a wood-fired kitchen offering an array of inventive sandwiches and pizzas, such as the Nuevo Aloha, which pairs prosciutto and pineapple with pickled jalapeños.

GOOD TO KNOW Check the status at the Mothership location before making the trek. *Mothership: 20 ABC Mesa Road, El Prado. Taos Taproom: 201 Paseo del Pueblo Sur; (575) 758–1900. taosmesabrewing.com.*

The Enchanted Circle

New Mexico's Enchanted Circle, a National Forest Scenic Byway, winds eighty-four miles through some of the state's most dramatic backdrops, including 13,161-foot Wheeler Peak in the Sangre de Cristos. Along the way, you'll find ski hills, hiking trails, lakes and rivers, historic sites, and a handful of adorable mountain towns, which provide places to pause and soak up the views and vibes, and to perhaps enjoy some hoppy refreshments. If you're traveling clockwise from Taos onto State Road 38, the first such stop is the RED RIVER BREWING COMPANY, a surprisingly robust operation with twelve rotating taps. This sprawling, two-story hangout offers an outsize menu featuring rib eyes and salmon as well as burgers and sandwiches of all varieties. And here's a bonus: The brewery also distills a line of spirits, including vodka, gin, and a spiced rum, as well as its own nonalcoholic root beer. *217 W. Main Street; (575) 754–4422; redriverbrewing.com.*

Around the bend in Eagle Nest is COMANCHE CREEK BREWING COMPANY, which was established in a tiny cabin built in 1910 and only recently moved to a slightly less tiny cabin. Folks rave about the brews here as well as the views of the Sangre de Cristos. *5 Comanche Creek Road. (575) 377–2337; comanchecreekbrewingco.com.*

Stay the course past Eagle Nest Lake to Angel Fire's ENCHANTED CIRCLE BREWING. A popular post–Angel Fire Resort respite, this spot offers hearty pub food and a great beer lineup of twenty or so rotating options (using locally sourced mountain water and hops), including the much-lauded Black Lake Bourbon Vanilla Porter. Check out the Albuquerque taproom at 6001 San Mateo Blvd. NE (505-615-5446), which serves food too. *20 Sage Lane. (505) 216–5973; enchantedcircle brewing.com.*

Just remember, kids: *No drinking and driving.*

Santa Fe

TOP PICK

Santa Fe Brewing Company

From the moment I saw SFB's yellow New Mexican flag cans containing Happy Camper IPA, I was hooked on this brewery. But go below the surface of our state's oldest (founded in 1988) and biggest (forty thousand barrels annually) brewery, and you'll find beer experiences that are worth going beyond the can. For instance, the Beer Hall at HQ, a two-story hangout that opened in early 2020, is a sublime place to enjoy a brew and a New Mexico sunset. Across the dirt parking lot is The Bridge, where indie bands perform and you can dance under a blanket of a zillion stars. Closer to the plaza, the Brakeroom, housed inside a building once occupied by railroad brakemen, has a Victorian vibe inside and a twinkly romantic one outside, where picnic benches sit beneath strings of lights. Go into nearly any New Mexico market and you can pick up those ubiquitous Zia cans (plus others, such as the Java Stout, which provides a shot of caffeine).

GOOD TO KNOW There's a tap house at the Green Jeans Food Hall (3600 Cutler Avenue NE, 505–881–0887) in Albuquerque. *7 Caliente Road; (505) 466–6938. 510 Galisteo Road; (505) 780–8648. 35 Fire Place; (505) 424–3333. santafebrewing.com.*

Albuquerque

Bow and Arrow Brewing Company

There's something different about this brewery and taproom. First of all, the aesthetic: While we've grown accustomed to the edgy-industrial brewery finish, there's a warmth here among the barrels and tanks, where light-stained picnic table seating and simple circular chandeliers contrast with the natural wood–paneled walls and exposed ceiling ducts. This also is the first brewery owned by Native American women, and it's rapidly becoming a locals' favorite, and not just for its tasty

Santa Fe Brewing Company is one of the state's biggest, with multiple taprooms and a ubiquitous presence at liquor stores throughout New Mexico.

brews—the vibe here is "chill New Mexico." Founders Shyla Sheppard, who grew up on the Fort Berthold Reservation in North Dakota and is a member of the Three Affiliated Tribes, and Missy Begay, a Diné born in Albuquerque, combined their business skills and marketing and design know-how, and out of the hops has arisen a product and a place that captures what a brewery should be about: good community and great beer. Food trucks roll up daily, and the brewery offers a strong selection of bottles you can take with you and enjoy at home. (Might I suggest the Bolos and Bling Brett IPA?)

GOOD TO KNOW Good news for the Four Corners folks: Bow and Arrow opened a taproom in Farmington in 2020. *608 McKnight Avenue NW. (505) 247–9800; bowandarrowbrewing.com.*

Canteen Brewhouse

Sometimes it's good to be the old dog in the room. With more than twenty-five years and several Great American Beer Fest awards under its brewing belt—and claiming the title of the longest-standing brewery in Albuquerque (opening in 1993)—Canteen has earned its stripes. It captures the spirit of the first-wave neighborhood craft breweries, with its kid- and dog-friendly atmosphere; pseudo-industrial decor; well-established brewpub menu with pretzels, brats, and other favorites; and a solid brew lineup that includes superb IPAs and a husky but relaxed stout. And with the taproom location opened in 2016 on Tramway en route to the Sandia Tram, it's safe to say that this place has plenty more years in its future.

GOOD TO KNOW Check out free live music on Thursdays and Sundays. *2381 Aztec Road NE; (505) 881–2737. 417 Tramway Boulevard NE; (505) 200–2344. canteenbrewhouse.com.*

Ex Novo Brewing Company

This brewery's Mass Ascension IPA almost immediately stole my heart. And my first sip came from a can! Second choice, when I want to dial it back a bit, is the Perle Haggard Pils. The experience is made even better by going to the source, a sweet little three-acre spread in the upscale farming community of Corrales, a slow-paced, alpaca-populated slice of the bosque just north of Albuquerque. This brewery is actually a Portland import, but Corrales native Joel Gregory, founder of Ex Novo, decided to bring it all back home. The brewery's mission is to donate all profits to charities, which makes drinking these beers all the sweeter.

GOOD TO KNOW There's no food here, but patrons can hit up food trucks and nearby restaurants and bring in food to enjoy on the outdoor patio. *4895 Corrales Road, Corrales. (505) 508-0547; exnovo brew.com.*

Tractor Brewing Company

This is Albuquerque's old guard, starting in 1999 in Los Lunas before moving to downtown Albuquerque. This brewing mainstay now has five locations; the latest opened in its original hometown of Los Lunas. The beers are all extremely competent, and the brewery has expanded into hard ciders and spirits. Both the Wells Park and Los Lunas locations have beer-friendly menus, while the others are near food trucks or neighborhood eateries serving stuff you can bring into the taprooms. Los Lunas and Wells Park offer creative cocktails based on the brewery's distilling label, Troubled Minds Distilling.

GOOD TO KNOW Tractor founded Beer for a Better Burque to provide a means for giving back to local charitable organizations. *1800 Fourth Street NW; (505) 243-6752. 118 Tulane Drive SE; (505) 433-5654. 5720 McMahon Boulevard NW; (505)*

361-1834. 470 Sandsage Street, Los Lunas; (505) 205-4789. getplowed.com.

Tin Can Alley Albuquerque

This hip hangout became the city's second shipping container development when it opened in 2020, following in the footsteps of its popular sister property, Green Jeans Food Hall. The containers have a chic-rustic vibe with their concrete floors, large murals by local artists, and upcycled materials that make up seating and service spaces. This 11,000-square-foot incarnation in Northeast Albuquerque and Green Jeans share many tenants, a popular one being the Santa Fe Brewing Company taproom. You'll also find coffee, pizza, handcrafted ice cream, and other treats. *tincanalley abq.com.*

Las Cruces

High Desert Brewing Company

Today's college students have no idea how good they have it. With a plethora of pubs and breweries where they can hang out, play games, study, bring their dogs, and—here's a biggie—drink some really good handcrafted beers—these are indeed the salad days. High Desert Brewing came on the scene in 1997 as an offshoot of the local community of home brewers, and while I wouldn't call it a college hangout, it was the only place where beerophiles could gather and help spread the gospel that there was more out there than Coors Light. Tucked into an older neighborhood, High Desert eschews a hipster vibe and manages to be collegial, comfortable, and friendly, like the man cave of your favorite uncle who also happens to be a top-notch brewer. The beer offerings have had ample time to mature and expand; High Desert now produces more than twenty brews, including some award-winning IPAs (as well as a popular homemade root beer).

GOOD TO KNOW The food here is pretty good (a roster of fried stuff, burgers, and pretzels), and musicians stop by a couple of times each week. *1201 W. Hadley Avenue. (575) 525–6752; highdesertbrewingco.com.*

Icebox Brewing Company

Some folks I've shared a beer with here remember when this aptly named tin-wrapped taproom was actually an icehouse. That's what's great about watching your hometown grow up: Today, we have devices that chill our food and deliver ice cubes on demand, but when we can repurpose a place from our past and do something "cool" with it, what could be better? This up-and-coming brewery, which opened in 2019, is one to watch. The brews are made on-site and are superb (I really dig the Double Milkshake IPA), and a strong element of Las Cruces pride permeates. (The massive black-and-white mural of the Organ Mountains behind the bar helps.)

GOOD TO KNOW Check out the lively taproom at 3231 N. Main Street; (575) 556–9517. The taco taproom Boneyard Cantina opened in summer 2020 near downtown at 139 Main Street; (575) 800–5967. *2825 W. Picacho Avenue; (575) 526–7129. iceboxbrewing.com.*

Spotted Dog Brewery

The small village of Mesilla got its first craft brewery when home brewer Jerry Grandle and wife, Susan, opened up this compact but popular spot in 2014. The brews are unfiltered and tasty, and they pair well with the creative menu that rotates weekly. The Hatch mac and cheese and the poutine are always tempting, but it takes a lot to pull me away from the Dog's green chile cheeseburger with beer-battered fries.

GOOD TO KNOW Dogs are allowed on the patio, where you can sip, eat, and enjoy views of the Organ Mountains. *2920 Avenida de Mesilla. (575) 650–2729; spotted dogbrewery.com.*

This "cool" brewery is housed in a former icehouse in Las Cruces and has opened other taprooms in the city.

Dogs feel at home on the Spotted Dog Brewery patio, where owners can enjoy brews, burgers, and views of the Organ Mountains.

I married a man who grew up in the small southeastern town of Lovington, and no one was more surprised than he when the Drylands Brewing Company opened up in this town of eleven thousand people in 2017 (near the Methodist church, no less). We weren't sure what to expect of a microbrewery in this practically dry town, but to my surprise, the beer and the food are superb—even the town teetotalers frequent this place. The staple brick oven–fired pizzas are bubbly and flavorful, and there's a gluten-free crust option, another oddity in this pump jack and ranching part of the country. Even better? The IPA holds its own, and the pilsner is light and refreshing.

A city-size population helps but isn't necessarily required for a town to support New Mexico's booming craft brew industry. Breweries and brewpubs are bubbling up all over the state—and in some instances have been hiding in plain sight. In New Mexico, our creative types tend to merge with science types to form mighty fine collaborations. So in towns where bars are often hard to find, brewpubs have emerged as a social scene, offering good food, beer if you want it, and a hub for wholesome family fun and entertainment. Get a flight to find your favorite and then settle in and enjoy what the brewery and the townsfolk have to offer.

Following is a twelve-pack of brew towns worth the stop.

1. Farmington, Three Rivers Eatery and Brewhouse
Take your pick of places to eat and drink on this town block that includes the brewery, a restaurant with a top-notch green chile cheeseburger (see the "Green Chile Cheeseburger" chapter) and other entrées, a taproom that serves an extensive lineup of pizzas and subs, and a distillery offering such sophisticated appetizers as charcuterie and Korean-influenced dishes. *101 E. Main Street. (505) 324–2187; threeriversbrewery.com.*

2. Embudo/Española, Blue Heron Brewing Company
This woman-owned brewery opened in 2009 and is still going strong with two taprooms. The Embudo room sits right next to the Río Grande in one of the prettiest little nooks in northern New Mexico. A restaurant inside the Española location serves killer pizzas, chicken wings (that sauce!), and some surprisingly cosmopolitan Italian dishes. *Española: 100 Los Alamos Highway; (505) 747–4506. Embudo: 2214 State Highway 68; (505) 579–9188. blueheronbrews.com.*

3. Los Alamos, Bathtub Row Brewing Co-op
Some of the most brilliant science minds in the world have lived or live in this

Even New Mexico's small towns get the brews.

secluded mesa-top town, birthplace of the Manhattan Project and current home of Los Alamos National Laboratory. So all offerings, from food to parks, have been well planned and thought out, including the town's only brewery and taproom, operated as a co-op (meaning the brewery sells memberships) and serving as a gathering place for this tight-knit community. Named for a street with a stretch of homes featuring bathtubs, a rarity during the 1940s, this is a superb place to end a day after exploring Manhattan Project National Historical Park sites or nearby Bandelier National Monument. *163 Central Park Square. (505) 500–8381; bathtubbrewing.coop.*

4. Jemez Springs, Second Alarm Brewhouse
Albuquerqueans try to keep this beautiful pocket of New Mexico a secret from the rest of us, but we are finding it, thanks to a quest to hike volcanic terrain, soak in some scenic hot springs, and, yes, enjoy beer and food in the process. Tucked inside a historic firehouse in this tiny village is a strong selection of beers brewed on-site as well as other New Mexico taps, plus an extensive menu of tacos, sandwiches, and appetizers. *17691 State Highway 4. (575) 829–4222; second-alarm-brewhouse.business.site.*

5. Portales, Roosevelt Brewing Company
Pub food and good craft brews make for some of the best surprises about Portales, which is also known for its peanut farms, the well-regarded Eastern New Mexico University (go Greyhounds!), major archaeological sites, and a windmill museum. This popular brewery serves up an expansive rotating roster of tasty ales, lagers, and bocks (among others) as well as wood-fired, sourdough-crust pizzas and burgers (bison or beef). *201 S. Main Street. (575) 226–2739; rooseveltbrewing.com.*

The beers pair perfectly with pizzas and other entrées at Blue Heron Brewing Company in Española.

Not ready to commit? Sample the wares
with a flight from Cloudcroft Brewing
Company.

6. Truth or Consequences, Truth or Consequences Brewing Company

As T or C is gateway for Spaceport America, about thirty miles southeast of town, it was of utmost importance that this small town open a brewery. Mission accomplished, and even if you aren't planning to plop down a few hundred grand to fly to the edge of space, you might want to make the drive here to try the brews. There's no food but often a nearby food truck as well as occasional live music. In case you can't get to T or C, the brewery opened a taproom in Las Cruces in early 2020 at 2001 E. Lohman Avenue; (575) 222–4986. *410 N. Broadway Street. (575) 297–0289; torcbeer.com.*

The brews and decor have an oil industry theme at the Wellhead Restaurant and Brewpub in Artesia.

7. Silver City, Little Toad Creek Brewery and Distillery
Good beers, spirits, food, and music come together at this lively hangout that opened in 2013 in downtown Silver City. (Read more in the

wine and spirits chapter.) I favor the Smart Blond Ale (I wonder why), which is best paired with the green chile fried chicken. *200 N. Bullard Street. (575) 956-6144; little toadcreek.com.*

8. Cloudcroft, Cloudcroft Brewing Company

Mountains town and microbrews are like peanut butter and jelly—they make each other better. This rambling cozy-cabin spot with a fireplace and live music also has a solid beer lineup and a blazingly spicy green chile pizza called the Zia Pie. Plus, there's a back patio for enjoying the mountain air and a steady stream of live music events. *1301 Burro Avenue. (575) 682-2337; cloudcroftbrewing.com.*

9. Lincoln, Bonito Valley Brewing Company

If Billy the Kid were alive today, he'd definitely be tempted to wet his whistle here. Tucked inside a charming old adobe in a town that was known for its lawlessness in the mid-1800s, Bonito Valley offers a limited number of brews (in addition to a few guest taps). The famous outlaw would no doubt be pleased to know there's an amber named in his honor. *692 Calle la Placita. (575) 653-4810; bonitovalleybrewing .com.*

10. Lovington, Drylands Brewing Company

Surprise! There's a brewery here. And the beers are great. The meatball appetizer is worth the drive too. *322 N. Main Street. (575) 739-2739; facebook.com /drylandsbrewingco.*

11. Artesia, Wellhead Restaurant and Brewpub

An array of oil and gas business signs cover the walls here, and the clientele includes its share of roughnecks (oil field workers). But the vibe in this office building–turned–microbrewery downtown is family-friendly and provides a good

Celebrate after exploring Carlsbad Caverns National Park or the nearby mountains with a tall cool one at Guadalupe Mountain Brewing Company.

entrée to those getting to know craft beers. *332 W. Main Street. (575) 746-0640; thewell headpub.com.*

12. Carlsbad

This town is hopping these days, which has led to the creation of two breweries in town: MILTON'S BREWING occupies a cool old building downtown and offers a series of beers inspired by musicians who've played there. *213 W. Mermod Street. (575) 725-5779; miltonsbrewing.com.* After you've trekked through the miles of trails traversing the depths of Carlsbad Caverns National Park, GUADALUPE MOUNTAIN BREWING COMPANY is the natural next stop. You'll find pizzas, panini, and a roster of good beers. (The Luscious IPA gets my vote.) *3324 National Parks Highway. (575) 887-8747; gmbrewingco.com.*

8 Salúd
Wineries and Distilleries

An immersive and pleasurable way to explore some of the best of what New Mexico has to offer is through its wineries. They tend to be friendly establishments, many with a rustic southwestern flair, and are often tucked in rural places that also are hotbeds for artists and other creative types. They're usually founded and run by families, some of whom have had wine-making in their blood for generations. Wine has been a staple on the New Mexico scene for close to four hundred years, thanks to monks who brought Mission grape plantings from Spain to make wine for sacramental purposes. Some of today's vintners have come to the craft organically, questing to get their hands dirty and, in the process, build spaces where people can come together, sip wines, and enjoy a stunning sunset.

Most of the grapes that go into New Mexico glasses have European pedigrees. But once southwestern waters have flowed through those vines, which are

New Mexico's wine history can be traced back nearly four hundred years to the arrival of the Spaniards.

rooted in sandy soil warmed by our sun, they produce grapes that are distinctly New Mexican. Perhaps most importantly, these chardonnays, tempranillos, and merlots often are poured for you by the person who shepherded the grapes throughout their journey. You can taste that.

Of course, not all these wineries are small operations. New Mexico has its share of players, putting the state on the (wine) map. Those in the Lordsburg–Deming area are even large enough to send their grapes within and across state borders to other wineries. New Mexico has three American viticultural areas—the Middle Rio Grande Valley, the Mimbres Valley, and the Mesilla Valley—which encompass more than twelve hundred acres, translating into more than a million cases of wine and many dozens of varietals.

Some of the bigger wineries boast Napa-style tasting rooms and charming cafés with menus that represent their lineage, offering quality wine-tasting experiences that rival those in more sophisticated wine-growing regions of the United States. Others are small roadside adobes tucked next to a river, with little more than a tiny sign pointing the way to the tasting room.

So how do you decide where to sample the wares and who's got the goods? Here's the best advice I've heard: "If you pass a winery, you should stop and try it, because you might find something you like," says Michele Padberg, a certified advanced sommelier and co-owner of Vivác Winery in Dixon in northern New Mexico. You will never regret taking the time to get to know a person, a family, or a community through one of its wineries.

Have a hankering for something stronger? We like our spirits too, and a vibrant distilling scene has been taking shape over the past decade or so.

While the tasting room experiences for spirits are less hoity-toity and more industrial hipster than the wine rooms, the founders are the same breed of enterprising, creative, and science-minded folks. And they are taking whiskeys, gins, vodkas, agave spirits, and others to lofty heights. As these spirits are still coming into their own and finding audiences, the distilleries are adding mixologists to the tasting room experience. The results are long menus filled with colorful craft cocktails that show off the spirits in ingenious ways, often incorporating regional ingredients.

New Mexico is home to more than fifty wineries and tasting rooms and more than a dozen distilleries, all of which have unique notes and qualities that make them worth the stop. So take Michele's advice: If you see a tasting room, stop in. Take a sip. Get to know the makers. And enjoy the New Mexico spirit that shines through.

The following is a trek through some of the state's top wineries and distilleries, as well as a few places where you can find a collection of many New Mexico–made beverages under one roof. Some offer superb sips, others feature friendly folks, and at others, it's all about the place.

Farmington

3 Rivers Eatery and Brewhouse

This is where grown-ups go to sip spirits in Farmington. This sophisticated room, accented with furniture and design elements handmade by owner John Silva, is a space I'd expect to find in a hip San Francisco or Denver 'hood. But here we are, in a relatively remote corner of New Mexico (one of four corners up here, as a matter of fact), in a room just a stone's throw from where the San Juan, Animas, and La Plata Rivers converge. The distillery at the back of this place makes gin, vodka, rum, whiskey, and agave, and then crafts a roster of highly civilized cocktails to showcase them. (My vote goes to the whiskey creations.) It's also one of the few places in town where you'll find tonkotsu ramen and other such exotic (for this area) items on a tapas menu. (Read more about 3 Rivers in the "Green

Sophisticated sippers chill at Farmington's 3 Rivers Brewstillery Lounge, which concocts cocktails from craft spirits distilled on-site.

Chile Cheeseburger" and "Craft Beer" chapters.)

GOOD TO KNOW Tours of the brewery and distillery are available and include tastings. *101 E. Main Street. (505) 324–2197; threeriversbrewery.com.*

Wines of the San Juan

This is what a New Mexico wine-tasting spot is all about. It's rustic, with hospitable winemaker hosts, set in a cottonwood-shaded bosque near the San Juan River, and, just for good measure, with a gaggle of peacocks strolling about. With a background in farming and ranching, owner David Arnold and his wife, Marcia Harris, purchased this property in 1999 and set about growing grapes and learning to make wines. Despite a steep learning curve, they've managed to develop a slate of wines that range from a rich, award-winning cabernet to a crisp, dry Riesling and more than a dozen other varietals in between.

GOOD TO KNOW Check the website for hours, as the winery often closes for weeks at a time during the winter months. *233 Highway 511, Blanco. (505) 632–0879; winesofthesanjuan.com.*

Dixon

La Chiripada

From the little white entrance arch to the beautiful vineyards that sweep across the property, this winery just makes me want to put it in my pocket and carry it with me wherever I go. The name is Spanish slang for "a stroke of luck," but La Chiripada's wines are no accident. Years of sweat equity and research have gone into the twenty varieties, which visitors can sip inside the little white adobe room that brothers Michael and Patrick Johnson built themselves in the 1980s (making this one of the oldest family-owned wineries in New

La Chiripada in Dixon produces about twenty types of wine, many of which can be sampled in the winery's cozy adobe tasting room.

Mexico). My picks here are the dolcetto, which has hints of smokiness, and the award-winning port.

GOOD TO KNOW Charming Dixon is worth the drive to explore its array of small artist studios. (The popular Dixon Studio Tour typically takes place in the fall.) *Highway 75 Road 1119. (505) 579–4437; lachiripada.com.*

Vivác Winery

As I sipped a crisp white, watching the sun drop behind mountains cradling a vineyard and the sliver of water that is Embudo Creek, I pondered what would make a flavorful Austrian Grüner Veltliner grape want to grow in New Mexico, so far from home. As the mountains turned purple and the temperature dropped, I realized that maybe here, it doesn't feel so homesick. Along with the mountain air, perhaps it's also because the grapes are so pampered under the care of owners and homegrown brothers Chris and Jesse Padberg and their wives, Liliana and Michele. Or maybe it's because once they go through the wine-making process and end up in a bottle, they get to sit next to wines made from other expat grapes, such as the Nebbiolo or the Petit Verdot. That's the life of the Vivác grape, and although it's not Europe, it's a pretty good life. Many of today's New Mexico winemakers take cues from their European and Californian counterparts, producing top wines that are holding their own in the industry. Visit them and you get to sit and sip in a place like Dixon, a quaint, one-main-road arts enclave that is one of New Mexico's most beautiful wine-growing pockets. For the Padbergs, wine-making is a family affair, done on land that's been in the family for generations but with a modern sensibility for sipping and food pairing.

GOOD TO KNOW You can also sample the wares at the Vivác tasting room at the Santa Fe Farmers Market Pavilion on Saturdays. *2075 State Highway 68. (505) 579-4441; vivacwinery.com.*

Taos

Rolling Still Distillery

Have I wandered into a Restoration Hardware showroom? Can't be, since someone just handed me a drink called the Honey Badger, made with locally distilled oregano honey–infused vodka. This modern, stylish hangout made me think I'd teleported to a hip San Francisco speakeasy, yet something about this room and the cocktails is distinctly northern New Mexican. Maybe it's the hospitality. Maybe it's drinks that bear such names as the Ruby Ristra (made with red chile–infused vodka) or the Macho Mule (red or green chile–infused vodka). The cocktails are strong, so the locally sourced snacks—try the locavore platter featuring beet deviled eggs, or the roasted pecans and pepitas in red chile and honey—are a handy accompaniment.

GOOD TO KNOW Pick up Rolling Still spirits at liquor stores throughout New Mexico. *110 Paseo del Pueblo Norte, Suite D. (575) 613-0326; rollingstill.com.*

Santa Fe

Santa Fe Spirits

Santa Fe is lucky that founder and whiskey lover Colin Keegan decided in 2010 to tackle the serious void in locally crafted spirits in the City Different. Another stroke of luck was that the Englishman was living in nearby Tesuque on an apple orchard, which also grew a fermentation boon. Over the past decade, Keegan has managed to build and grow his distillery to include production of my favorites, Colkegan Single Malt Whiskey (with malt smoked in mesquite) and Wheeler's Gin, a staple in my cabinet. If you like apple brandy, which I didn't think I did until I tasted this one, you'll love Santa Fe Spirits Apple Brandy, as well as the single malt whiskey finished in the apple brandy barrels. And again from the files of "I didn't think I would like this": the Atapiño Liqueur, made with roasted piñons soaked in Silver Coyote white whiskey and sweetened with ponderosa pine resin. Drink it straight in small sips or use it in a cocktail to prompt your guests to inquire, "What is in this amazing drink?"

The craft cocktails at Rolling Still Distillery in Taos are made with local ingredients and house-made spirits.

Santa Fe Spirits produces some of the state's most popular sips, which imbibers can sample at the distillery's small Santa Fe tasting room.

tonic, made with Tumbleroot's aromatic botanical gin, and from then on, it's been my go-to. I'm sure the Moscow Mule, the Paloma, and the glass-aged old-fashioned are delicious, but I may never know. (Okay, I do know, and they are great.) Drink a fancy cocktail here or pick up a bottle to go. Stay for the music, have a burger, or just hang out under the shade trees, where you can sip as you watch the kiddos play on the slide and the sun slip away on a perfect Santa Fe day. (Read more in the "Craft Beer" chapter.)

GOOD TO KNOW The production facility at a separate location has a small tasting room at 320 Bisbee Court, so sippers can see the tanks and stills where the magic is made. *2791 Agua Fria Street. (505) 780–5730; tumblerootbreweryanddistillery.com.*

Las Vegas

Bar Castaneda

Thankfully for all of us craft cocktail lovers, Andrew Szeman, the bar manager here, "loves everything booze." He speaks fluently and fluidly about all things adult-beverage oriented, so you can order anything on the craft menu with the confidence that it's been tested, tasted, and certified delicious. A rotating menu plays with a variety of ingredients and combos for the house specialties, but you'll also find well-made takes on the classics. Szeman is a rum master, so ask him about his favorite concoctions, which go well beyond the basic daquiri. (Read more in the "Green Chile Cheeseburger" chapter.)

GOOD TO KNOW The bar is located inside Hotel Castaneda, a historic Harvey House hotel that catered to train passengers in the early 1900s. "Fredheads" congregate here in November for the annual Fred Harvey History Weekend. *524 Railroad Avenue. (505) 434–1005; kinlvnm.com.*

All of this and more can be imbibed at the quaint adobe tasting room near the plaza, although many of these spirits are available wherever regional liquors are sold.

GOOD TO KNOW Visitors can book tours and classes through the website. *Downtown Tasting Room: 308 Read Street; (505) 780–5906. Distillery and Tasting Room: 7505 Mallard Way, Unit 1; (505) 467–8892. santafespirits.com.*

TOP PICK

Tumbleroot Brewery and Distillery

I thank Tumbleroot for my love of gin. We stopped here one lazy afternoon, needing a quick spot for a snack and refreshment with the kids before heading to the Santa Fe Airport. (Yes, Santa Fe has an airport.) I wasn't wanting beer, so I perked up at the cocktail menu, in which Tumbleroot's gins, vodkas, rums, whiskeys, and agave spirits get a starring role. I had a simple gin and

Albuquerque

Casa Rondeña Winery, Los Ranchos de Albuquerque

Resembling a Spanish–Moorish oasis, Casa Rondeña puts forth great effort to transport sippers to the European continent. Rows of vineyards provide a lush pattern of green, and if you score a seat overlooking the pond and tinkling fountains, you are going to question whether you're still in central New Mexico. I recommend just soaking it all up, especially with a glass of the full-bodied cabernet franc or the peachy viognier. It's surprising that founder and owner John Calvin is a native Albuquerquean, given that this winery is so essentially Spanish in both tone and bottle. But Calvin is a renaissance man, a world traveler who has lived in Spain and is also an accomplished guitarist. His sensibilities (as well as those of his wife, Christina Viggrano) have shaped this little piece of paradise for wine lovers.

Sip Here: The Legal Tender Saloon and Eating House, Lamy

It's part speakeasy, part Old West saloon, and part sophisticated eatery, the kind of place you go to celebrate a graduation or a have a memorable date. Perched in the heart of Lamy, a picturesque railroad town about twenty miles south of Santa Fe, Legal Tender has been greeting railroad passengers since it was built in 1881 to serve the Atchison, Topeka, and Santa Fe Railway. Its renovation in 2019 breathed new life into both this building, which is on the National Register of Historic Places, and the town of Lamy, where Amtrak delivers passengers arriving for Santa Fe. (The train doesn't go into Santa Fe.) The rambling dining rooms here are filled with art and artifacts depicting the romance of rail travel and make for a delightful place to chow down on the pecan-smoked ribs or the spicy Korean wings. But the bar is fast becoming a locals' favorite, with its ornate back bar and black-and-white tiled floor. My tip? Belly up to the bar, order a Sazerac, enjoy the local musicians, and revel in the northern New Mexico railroad spirit.

Lamy's Legal Tender is where craft cocktails meet New Mexico railroad history.

GOOD TO KNOW Open Fridays through Sundays; reservations recommended for dinner. The Santa Fe–based Chili Line Brewery opened a small taproom in the train station across the road and also serves a limited menu and craft beers. *151 Old Lamy Trail. (505) 466–1650; legaltenderlamy.com.*

Duke City Sips

The Albuquerque area has more than ten distilleries and tasting rooms, some of which are attached to breweries. The number continues to expand, thanks to receptive audiences who more and more are seeking spirits that are well crafted, homegrown, and in many cases made with ingredients plucked from our local deserts and mountains. Always inquire about taking a tour, as most of them offer a peek behind the scenes.

A good start is **BROKEN TRAIL SPIRITS AND BREW**, which has a tasting room in Uptown Albuquerque. The spirits reflect the founders' love of the outdoors and are made with locally sourced ingredients. My favorite here is the Tres Pistolas Bourbon. *6902 Menaul Boulevard NE. (505) 221-6281; brokentrailspirits.com.*

STILL SPIRITS, located downtown, serves cocktails made with its own spirits (including some creative vodka infusions), offering an alternative place to imbibe in this brewery-heavy part of town. *120 Marble Avenue NW. (505) 750-3138; facebook.com/stillspiritsabq.*

LEFT TURN DISTILLING serves distinctive spirits—such as a blue corn whiskey and a piñon rum—as well as an extensive menu of tacos and burgers from The Kitchen. Bloody Marys are featured on occasional Sundays, when you can choose which toppings to stack in your glass. *2924 Girard Boulevard NE. (505) 508-0508; leftturndistilling.com.*

Located inside a former National Cash Register building downtown, the **SAFE HOUSE DISTILLING COMPANY** makes a well-crafted vodka (other spirits are in the works) and cool cocktails in a distinct tasting room with long tables and dark walls. *616 Gold Avenue SW. safehousedistillingco.com.*

GOOD TO KNOW Open daily from noon to 7 p.m. *733 Chavez Road NW. (505) 344-5911; casarondena.com.*

Gruet Winery

Prepping for New Year's Eve? Stock up on Demi Sec. Anniversary? Cuvée Laurent Extended Tirage Rosé. Brunch? Blanc de Noirs. There's a sip for every occasion at this big-time, third-generation winery that has managed to make its way into the hearts of all of us who love the bubbly. The tasting room in Albuquerque is a beautiful spot to sit and learn how sparkling wines are made and why these grapes have become so popular. There's no food here, so BYO cheese.

Gruet Winery makes New Mexico's most popular sparkling wines.

GOOD TO KNOW The additional tasting room in Santa Fe at 210 Don Gaspar (505-989-9463) is a compact but beautiful spot to meet and sip. *8400 Pan American Freeway NE. (505) 821-0055; gruetwinery.com.*

Escape: Los Poblanos Historic Inn and Organic Farm

Chic French farmhouse meets rustic New Mexico at this sprawling farm laden with storied buildings and architectural beauty. Cats and guinea fowl roam freely as alpacas poke their curious heads up at visitors strolling by. An on-site bakery and gift shop sells all manner of kitchen items and foods designed to make you look and feel like a serious home cook. The restaurant, Campo, takes field-to-fork concepts seriously, and all the dishes incorporate New Mexico–made products—from the coffee beans and blue corn flour to the balsamic vinegar and cheeses. My favorite meal here is breakfast, because if I'm here that early it probably means I got to spend a night in one of the dreamy rooms that overlook the lavender fields or flower-filled courtyards. And then there's the cocktails at Bar Campo, many of them incorporating New Mexico–made spirits and infusions of the lavender and other herbs grown on-site. The Lavender '99, made with Wheeler's Gin from Santa Fe Spirits, sparkling wine, crème de violette, and of course lavender, is one of the most beautiful cocktails to ever pass the lips.

GOOD TO KNOW The inn hosts music, yoga, art and architecture tours, and special pairing dinners throughout the year. *4803 Rio Grande Boulevard NW, Los Ranchos de Albuquerque. (505) 344-9297; lospoblanos.com.*

D. H. Lescombes Winery introduced French grapes to the farmlands in Deming and Lordsburg.

Las Cruces

D. H. Lescombes Winery and Las Cruces Bistro

When this place opened on Avenida de Mesilla in the early 2010s, I remembered thinking, "Who the heck would open a winery in Las Cruces?" It turns out, one of state's most prolific winemakers, D. H. Lescombes, that's who. He had a vision for upping southern New Mexico's wining and dining game by extending his reach beyond his vineyards near Deming and adding a French touch. He did that by planting and propagating massive acres of vineyards east of Deming and through his talent as a winemaker. His first bistro reminded us that a little brie and chardonnay can break up a steady diet of red and green chile, and he built statewide followings with another bistro in Albuquerque and tasting rooms in

Deming and Santa Fe. The bistro's cuisine might not be French per se, but it does pair well with Lescombes's wine offerings, from rosés and petit syrahs to cabs and merlots. Plus, there's music most weekends as well as dog-friendly "yappy hours" every third Wednesday in the summer.

GOOD TO KNOW The winery offers guided tours, which include lunch at the Las Cruces bistro and VIP tasting at the Deming winery. *1720 Avenida de Mesilla. (575) 524-2408; lescombeswinery.com.*

Dry Point Distillery

If you had told me that at some point in my adult life I'd be sitting in a distillery sipping a bourbon cocktail with spirits made here in my hometown, I would've dropped my glass. But here I am, ordering a bourbon-based concoction called a Stray Dog, enjoying the fruits of the ingenuity of fellow Las Cruceans Stefan and Chris Schaefer. The father–son team opened this place in 2018. The cocktails are creative and fun and employ many local herbs and ingredients. Several rely on infusions of chile and other ingredients, especially in the vodka. And these small-batch spirits are worth having in your liquor cabinet too. My favorite is the Monsoon Gin—and not just for the great pen-and-ink rabbit on the label but also because its soft juniper edge is refreshing and smooth, especially in a gin and tonic.

GOOD TO KNOW Call for hours, which vary. *1680 Calle de Alvarez, Suite C2. (575) 652-3414; drypointdistillersnm.com.*

Mesilla

NM Vintage Wines Tasting Room

I literally stumbled into this room one hot summer day while exploring the Historic Mesilla Plaza. It took my eyes a few minutes to adjust, but when they did, I thought I'd wandered into a romantic Mexican cantina. With the saltillo tile floors, rustic furniture, exposed brick wall, and hand-blown glassware, I was also pretty sure I was home. The menu at this surprising little wine bar goes deep into New Mexico vintages and also includes sangrias, New Mexico craft beers and ciders, and a cheese plate featuring locally made and influenced cheeses. You'll also find a cigar menu as well as a roster of live entertainment that is best enjoyed with a glass of New Mexico red on the small patio out back.

GOOD TO KNOW Closed Mondays and Tuesdays. *2461 Calle de Principal. (575) 523-9463; nmvintagewines.com.*

Hillsboro

Black Range Vineyards

Hillsboro is technically a ghost town, with a population of fewer than 150 and a little collection of historic buildings left over from New Mexico's mining heyday in the 1880s. But it's pretty lively inside the tasting room, which sits amid towering cottonwoods that hang over Highway 152 as it slices through town. For most people, it's a stop en route to Silver City, about fifty-seven miles west, but it's a worthwhile one. The wines are pretty good, and owners Nicki and Brian O'Dell make you feel welcome among the small bar and couches. While I sipped a lovely syrah, a gentleman rode up on his bike, happy to see an oasis serving New Mexico beers too, as he had just experienced some serious mountainous terrain in this section of his cross-country ride. A few locals popped in and out, and I wistfully soaked up this slice of old New Mexico as we left the winery and peeked into the handful of shops that now occupy the old brick and adobe buildings resisting the pull of time and weather. While Hillsboro may never return to its glory days, the

opposite The Black Range Vineyards tasting room in Hillsboro is a peaceful place to try local grapes.

winery is a reminder of the value of taking the time to stop and enjoy a glass of locally made wine and visit with some strangers.

GOOD TO KNOW Open noon to 6 p.m. Thursday through Sunday. *10701 Highway 152. (575) 895–5000; blackrangevineyards .com.*

Silver City

La Esperanza Vineyard and Winery

Looking for a good picnic spot? Grab some artisan cheese and crackers and cut a path to La Esperanza Winery, where you can set up on the outside tables and enjoy views of the vines and the valley tucked into the mountains. Husband and wife David and Esperanza Gurule have been growing grapes and making wines for about ten years, and he enjoys the heck out of it. His Montepulciano won an award at the 2016 Finger Lakes International Wine Competition, and the pinot noir grapes are very happy at this cool elevation. David, a former atomic energy engineer at the Department of Energy in Los Alamos, has about four acres, four thousand vines, and five varieties, but really, it's about the place and the people out here.

GOOD TO KNOW Open noon–6 p.m. Friday–Sunday. *100 Da La O, Sherman. (505) 259–9523; laesperanzavineyardand winery.com.*

Little Toad Creek Brewery and Distillery

Green chile vodka, you say? While some might argue that New Mexicans have finally taken it too far with the pepper, I would suggest you try Silver Toad's Green Chile

Cucumber Gimlet made with Diablo Verde vodka. (The Toad Creek Bloody Mary is worthy as well.) The Gila Rita, made with Little Toad Creek's TeGila Silver Agave, is a highly respectable entry into New Mexico's margarita lineup—not too sweet, not too strong, refreshing even in the dead of winter when we're supposed to be drinking only bourbon. There are plenty of other spirits and cocktails to try here, along with a delectable and varied menu. The green chile fried chicken (breaded in rice flour and smothered in a green chile vodka sauce) pairs well with Little Toad's craft beers. On most weekends, diners are treated to live music, often by local artists. (Read more in the "Craft Beer" chapter.)

GOOD TO KNOW Be sure to check out the Las Cruces location (119 N. Main Street, 575-556-9934). *200 N. Bullard Street. (575) 956–6144; littletoadcreek.com.*

La Esperanza Vineyard and Winery is tucked into a scenic pocket of southwestern New Mexico near the Gila Wilderness.

Deming

Lescombes Family Vineyards

Luckily for us, the grapes in this region are represented not only by the Italian winemakers at Luna Rossa but also by the French here at Lescombes. Originally from Burgundy, wine patriarch Hervé Lescombes brought his skills to our little pocket of the world in the 1980s and has built an empire of grapes, wines, and bistros that has spread to other corners of the state and beyond. The wine-tasting room in Deming is a delightful place to sample the wares, but the bistros in Las Cruces and Albuquerque have menus to match the wines. In Santa Fe, don't miss the Hervé Wine Bar, which is in a cavernous room near the plaza and offers a selection of bruschettas that pair nicely with Lescombes's crisp rosés. The winery's Soleil line of bottled mimosas is a guilty pleasure among New Mexicans who brunch. These bubbly beverages, definitely on the sweet side, include such flavors as pomegranate and pineapple and are readily available across the Unites States (so get that hollandaise ready).

GOOD TO KNOW Check the website for wine festivals hosted at the various locations. *1325 De Baca Road SE. (575) 546–1179; lescombeswinery.com.*

Luna Rossa Winery

I know this isn't the Italian countryside. I've been in winds whipping so hard here that I've had to fight to stand upright. There's no foodie scene like Sonoma's or wine train like Temecula, California's. It's just grapes—and lots of them. This arid stretch of New Mexico, part of the Mimbres Valley American Viticultural Area, is home to two thousand acres of vineyards and is loved by cabernet, tempranillo, syrah, and other grapes that dig the hot days, cool nights, and high elevations. This is where the hard work of New Mexico's wine growing is getting done, and

the wineries and tasting rooms are worth the trip. Here you can take a gander at all those growing vines and then drop by the tasting room, which has a Tuscan vibe but with occasional entertainment by cowboy poets and New Mexico musicians. I have a hard time picking a favorite wine here (I'd suggest a flight if this is your first experience), especially among the reds. If pressed, I'd go with the Nini, a blend of a variety of Italian grapes aged in oak for fifty-eight months.

GOOD TO KNOW In Las Cruces, the tasting room (1321 Avenida de Mesilla, 575–526–2484) also has a pizzeria, where the pies are cooked in a brick oven fired with Italian wood. The Messicana pizza is made with chiles grown on the winery's Deming farm. *3710 W. Pine Street. (575) 544–1160; lunarossa winery.com.*

Alamogordo

McGinn's Pistachioland, Heart of the Desert Pistachios and Wine

It's not all candy and giant nuts at these side-by-side attractions in the desert outside of Alamogordo. You'll also find wine tasting. Pistachioland is the larger of the two, but both offer decent wines and a pleasant place to chill for a bit. Bottled under the Arena Blanca label, McGinn wines are reasonably priced, and while some tend to be on the sweeter side, the semidry chardonnay ($16) and the cabernet sauvignon ($14) are both good sippers. Heart of the Desert grows seven varieties of grapes—the cabernet is my top pick here too. (All wines are in the $14–$20 range.) (Read more in the sweets chapter.)

GOOD TO KNOW Pistachioland offers tours of the orchards. *Pistachioland: 7320 Highway 54/70. (800) 368–3081; pistachioland.com. Heart of the Desert: 7288 Highway 54/70. (575) 434–0035; heartofthedesert.com.*

Ruidoso

Noisy Water Winery

This scenic little mountain town has a lot to offer: hiking in Sierra Blanca, pine-scented air, cozy cabins, and a picturesque downtown filled with shops, coffeehouses, eateries, and this popular winery. Owner Jasper Riddle hit on the right fruit notes when he opened Noisy Water in 2009 and has kept growing and pouring ever since. A few of the wines might be a bit gimmicky (Besito Caliente green chile wine and the Big Legs Red, to name a couple), but the award-winning Barrel Select Mourvedre and Dolcetto, among many others, show that this winemaker is serious about his grapes. The tasting room downtown is crafted in "Ruidoso cabin chic," accented with natural wood-slab tables and pine floors. Wine makes me crave cheese, a happy coincidence since a variety of locally made cheeses are sold here too.

GOOD TO KNOW Check out the additional tasting rooms in Santa Fe, Cloudcroft, and Red River. *2342 Sudderth Drive. (575) 257–9335; noisywaterwinery.com.*

Glencoe Distillery, Glencoe

What happens when a restauranteur/coffee fanatic and a fine furniture maker decide they want to open a distillery together? They make beautiful spirits, such as GlenWillis Applewood Smoked American Single Malt Whiskey, as well as a trio of infused vodkas and a popular gin. You can sample these and more, as well as a menu of craft cocktails, on select days at the distillery in Glencoe or at the tasting room and bar at the back of Sacred Grounds Coffee and Tea House in Ruidoso. I took a liking to the Moscow Mule, a minty refresher on a warm mountain day, and the GlenWillis old-fashioned made with blood orange was just smoky enough to warm up my innards. (Read more about Sacred Grounds in the sweets chapter.)

Spirits made at the Glencoe Distillery find their way into an array of craft cocktails at Ruidoso's Sacred Grounds Coffee and Tea House.

GOOD TO KNOW Open 1:30–6 p.m. Thursday–Saturday. *27495 US 70. (575) 430–2325.*

Roswell

Pecos Flavors Winery

While the owners of Pecos Flavors have a small vineyard and produce a few varietals, the gravitational pull you'll feel at this restaurant/gift shop/tasting room/deli is more toward the sheer number of New Mexico wines (and beers) they serve and sell here. The bistro, open for lunch and dinner, has a full menu, but those sandwiches are hard to beat. When I daydream about sandwiches (don't tell me you don't do that), it's usually about their turkey with green chile jelly and Havarti on grilled focaccia.

The bar at The Trinity in Carlsbad offers free tastings of New Mexico's Luna Rossa and Balzano wines.

GOOD TO KNOW Wine tastings are part of the offerings, and the expansive gift shop is stocked with New Mexico–made food stuffs ranging from salsa and spices to chocolate and cheeses. *412 W. Second Street. (575) 627–6265; pecosflavorswinery.com.*

Carlsbad

The Trinity

The restaurant at the Trinity, a charming hotel whose life began in 1892 as the First National Bank, serves a fine lasagna bolloco with green chile. Thanks to a trio of local businessmen who rescued the building from potential demolition and began to transform it in 2007, this property on the corner has evolved into a hub for those seeking a good meal, a cozy room, or a place to enjoy a beverage at an elaborate marble-topped bar. From 3 to 7 p.m. Wednesday through Saturday you can sample wines from the owners' nearby Balzano Winery as well as the cream of the crop from Deming-based Luna Rossa Winery.

GOOD TO KNOW Request Room 206, called the Safe Room. The 1,100-square-foot space includes the old bank vault, which has been turned into a media room. *201 S. Canal Street. (575) 234–9891; thetrinityhotel.com.*

9 The Sweet Road
Traditional Treats

Just because we love our savories here doesn't mean we don't have a sweet tooth. In New Mexico, we're known primarily for our sopaipillas and biscochitos, New Mexico's official state cookie. At many New Mexican restaurants, a free basket of sopaipillas and a bottle of honey often show up with your meal, no questions asked. Bags of cinnamon-dusted biscochitos are ubiquitous at holiday time, and when guests are asked to bring refreshments for a gathering, you can count on seeing these delicate little cookies next to the fruit punch.

The biscochito, New Mexico's official state cookie, comes in many flavors and forms.

New Mexicans can be fiercely protective of our methods of frying and baking these staples, and I've seen a few arguments erupt over the home cook who deigns to admit she's used vegetable shortening in her biscochito recipe rather than a much-preferred scoop of lard. In the sopaipilla category, you'll find variations on the same deep-fried foundation: Some emerge as dense and doughy while others emerge as crispy, poufy pockets. And all hail the restauranteurs with the foresight to hand out wet wipes with their sopaipillas for those of us who have trouble containing our honey.

But let us not confine ourselves to cookies and fried dough. New Mexico is also agriculturally suited for nut growing, and to understand the state's sweets is to know your P's: peanuts, pistachios, pecans, and piñons. Peanuts come from Portales, and pistachios have been thriving in Alamogordo since the mid-1970s, transforming a crop that was, up until then, a major import. Piñon harvesting represents important cultural traditions, and the fruits of the trees find their way into a variety of dishes throughout the state. Pecan orchards fill the fertile Mesilla Valley and provide ample opportunities for fans of the nut to find it in products ranging from pecan-flavored craft beer to pies.

And because of the strong melding and influence of Spanish, Mexican, and Native epicurean trends, we've developed a penchant for chocolate, which, at the hands of our skilled chocolate makers, is transformed into everything from beautiful bars and truffles to rich elixirs that make you feel like Mesoamerican royalty when you sip them from tiny pottery cups.

The following are some travel-worthy sweet stops around the state that should be part of any foodie outing.

Taos

Chokolá Bean to Bar

I probably don't have to sell you on the idea of craft chocolate, so I'll just throw out a couple of words: bean to bar, mousse, truffles, drinkable chocolate. Perched in a sweet spot amid the John Dunn Shops near Taos Plaza, this little café will woo you with the aromas of cacao going from raw bean to edible treat. Take a seat outside and people-watch as you partake in a cup of the lavender sipping chocolate. For me, the effects of drinking this elixir are similar to those I get when I drink a margarita: happy, content, full. There's a selection of mousses to try too, and they are rich and satisfying. If you're on the go, grab an award-winning

Belize Maya Mountain bar, which is 70 percent chocolate, or a chocolate whiskey tart.

GOOD TO KNOW It's not all high-brow dark chocolate for sophisticated palates; there are treats here for kids too, like milkshakes and other items. *106 Juan Largo Lane. (575) 779–6163; chokolabeantobar.com.*

Orlando's New Mexican Café

Yes, you're going to be skeptical when I suggest you try avocado pie. But trust me, you're going to like it (even if you don't like avocados). This light green, slightly frozen treat is New Mexico's answer to Florida's key lime pie, with avocados that provide a creamy base and enlivened with just the right hints of lime and sweetness. At the top is a smidge of whipped cream, and on

above Chokolá Bean to Bar in Taos serves chocolate in several forms, from elixirs to mousse.

left Orlando's New Mexican Café in Taos serves a smooth and creamy avocado pie.

GHOST RANCH EDUCATION AND RETREAT CENTER Picture this: A woman in a simple dress, standing over a plein air canvas, her salt-and-pepper hair pulled into a tight bun and her face shaded by the ample brim of her hat. She looks out over the distant valley to Cerro Pedernal, a dramatic, flat-topped mountain, the result of ancient volcanic activity that left marks throughout this land. Around her, mountains have been peeled away to reveal layers of oranges and peaches and scorched reds that no one knew existed in rock formations. Visitors can step into the mind's eye of the enigmatic artist Georgia O'Keeffe, who lived part-time in a small house on the property here and prolifically painted the desert, sky, and mountains that surrounded her. Ghost Ranch was where O'Keeffe came in 1934, but there's more here than the artist's stamp. The facility offers workshops, classes, overnight accommodations, horseback trail rides, spiritual retreats, specialized tours, and hiking trails. In addition, the Florence Hawley Ellis Museum of Anthropology shows the history and impact of ancient humans in the area, and the Ruth Hall Museum of Paleontology highlights dinosaur discoveries. *ghostranch.org.*

THE O'KEEFFE: WELCOME CENTER, ABIQUIÚ HOME AND STUDIO TOUR Start your visit to this area at this architecturally stunning welcome center, where you'll find a sampling of O'Keeffe art, exhibits, and a gift shop, as well as the starting point for a tour of the artist's nearby home and studio. On the tour, you'll be immersed in the minimalist aesthetic that O'Keeffe maintained, from her simple but utilitarian kitchen to her stark white studio. Visitors can gaze down at the winding roads and river that O'Keeffe enjoyed and meander through her garden, which is still maintained and watered from an acequia. Advance reservations required. *okeeffemuseum.org.*

ECHO AMPHITHEATER HELLO . . . hello . . . hello. This popular locals' picnicking spot just three miles west of Ghost Ranch is home to a hollowed-out natural feature that makes for good echoes as well as hiking and exploring. A paved interpretive trail winds into Echo Canyon in the Carson National Forest, through scenic high-desert vegetation and up to some picturesque picnic tables. $2 entry fee. *fs.usda.gov.*

ABIQUIÚ LAKE This beautiful reservoir at the foot of Cerro Pedernal, covering fifty-two hundred acres on its surface, offers camping, boating, swimming, an interpretive center, and O'Keeffe-worthy views of surrounding red, pink, and white sandstone formations. *recreation.gov/camping/gateways/27.*

the bottom is a graham cracker crust that gives the pie a slightly salty finish. You're welcome. (Read more in the "Green and Red" chapter.)

GOOD TO KNOW The wait times can be long here, but you can grab a drink and sit by the outdoor fire pit while you await your table. *1114 Don Juan Valdez Lane. (575) 751–1450; facebook.com/orlandosnew mexicancafe.*

Sugar Nymphs Bistro, Peñasco

Sometimes it's nice to enjoy a simple piece of cake after a meal. Or between meals. Or for breakfast. Thankfully, you can experience all of the above here. After touring the galleries and wineries of the darling village of Dixon to the west, seek nourishment at this little gem of an eatery, which serves a range of dishes (brunch, lunch, and dinner), from goat cheese salad and a green chile black bean burger to a ginger and soy–marinated pork chop and grilled Angus rib eye. But the triple-layer chocolate cake, with its creamy fudgy frosting, is always where you'll find your heart.

GOOD TO KNOW Hours change with the seasons and occasionally with the weather. Call ahead or check the website before you hit the road. *15046 State Road 75. (575) 587–0311; sugarnymphs.com.*

Taos Cow Ice Cream and Deli, Arroyo Seco

It's hard to mess up ice cream, right? I would argue that it's equally challenging to really rise above the standard. After all, ice cream is basically cream, sugar, and other flavorings. But somehow, Taos Cow manages to emerge from the herd. Maybe it's because handcrafted ice creams are somewhat of a rarity in this part of chilly New Mexico. Part of the success comes from using the very best natural ingredients you can find and then leaning into the flavors that New Mexico does well, such as pistachio white chocolate (made with Alamogordo nuts), pecan nougat (made with Las Cruces–grown pecans), and crowd favorite Cherry Ristra, a blend of white, dark, and milk chocolate chunks with cherry ice cream. Believe me, these are all crave-able, even in winter when there's snow on the ground and skiing on the brain.

GOOD TO KNOW Taos Mountain Roasters provides the beans for lattes and other caffeinated treats. *483 New Mexico Highway 150. (575) 776–5640; mcoc6262.wixsite.com /taoscow.*

Santa Fe

Art of Chocolate, Cacao Santa Fe

The aroma of chocolate hits you in the face as soon as you walk into this somewhat generic location, tucked into the industrial, less sexy side of Santa Fe. But once you

At Santa Fe's Art of Chocolate, visitors can watch how cacao beans become edible and beautiful treats.

come to the counter area and realize that this is where the magic happens, you'll be transported to a Central American café. The emphasis at this 3,000-square-foot bean-to-bar shop and factory is on elixirs (drinking chocolates), beautiful truffles, and high-quality bars sourced from the best cacao beans. Mesoamerican-style elixirs are made with chiles, blue corn, florals, and spices, while a European side of the elixir menu focuses on mixing 100 percent chocolate with lavender and citrus. All the elixirs are delicious and somewhat intoxicating. The handcrafted chocolates are as beautiful as they are satisfyingly luscious. The round ones painted like Chaco pottery shards make excellent New Mexico–themed gifts.

GOOD TO KNOW Get elbows-deep into the art of chocolate-making by checking out the shop's classes, tastings, and tours. *3201 Richards Lane. (505) 471–0891; cacaosantafe.com.*

Chainé Cookie Shop

The macarons displayed in this artistic little bakery resemble an organized artist's palette, with rows of pinks, light greens, yellows, and creams. Those colors represent delicious flavors, such as strawberry rosé, Meyer lemon, and hazelnut latte, and you will struggle to settle on a favorite. This shop, operated by Chainé Peña, a sixth-generation New Mexican and baker, has carved out a sweet space. The pink floors and minimalist, feminine decor provide a civilized break from the Southwest aesthetic that tends to dominate the other Santa Fe Plaza shops. But the New Mexico flavors run deep and the treats are topnotch, so grab a couple of churro-flavored macarons or piñon chocolate chip cookies and a fresh-brewed latte, and sample something different in the City Different.

GOOD TO KNOW Open Tuesday–Saturday. *131 W. Water Street. (505) 570–4496; chainescookies.com.*

The sweets are works of art at Chainé Cookie Shop near the Santa Fe Plaza.

Kakawa Chocolate House

Remember when you were a kid and all you wanted to do was pour Hershey's chocolate syrup directly down your throat? That's the level of satisfaction achieved when you sit with a small Talavera cup in the cozy Kakawa adobe, just off the Santa Fe Plaza, and slurp the café's dense, warm, chocolate elixirs. Sippers will find a few concoctions to choose from, all based on ancient chocolate-making techniques and recipes that incorporate a range of herbs and other ingredients. I always feel a little buzz after sitting and drinking, and the friendly folks here are always willing to share the history and techniques behind their elixirs (and provide samples). The shop makes and sells truffles, caramels, and bars too, and you can pick up the mixes to make the elixirs at home.

GOOD TO KNOW The shop also sells ice cream. *1050 Paseo de Peralta; (505) 982–0388. 1300 Rufina Circle; (505) 930–5460. kakawachocolates.com.*

Shake Foundation

The cool and creamy concoctions served here are dubbed Adobe Mud Shakes, and, yes, your eyes might bulge out of your skull as you try to draw the ice cream through the straw. But once it melts to the perfect consistency, you're rewarded with a nostalgic blast of cold cream that'll take you back to your childhood. Go traditional with the vanilla, chocolate, or raspberry options or branch out to the lavender, coffee, or salted caramel. There are tasty ice cream scoops too, and all ingredients, from dairy and eggs to fruit toppings, are organic.

GOOD TO KNOW Parking is limited, and the lines are long during the summer, so aim for off-peak hours. Oh, and try the banana ice cream—it's amazing. *631 Cerrillos Road. (505) 988–8992; shakefoundation .com.*

Madrid

Shugarman's Little Chocolate Shop

In a funky town of colorful shops filled with art, books, cowboy boots, and coffee, with a dash of mining and movie history (*Wild Hogs* was filmed here), this tiny but mighty chocolate shop fits right in. Owner Harvey Shugarman's love of chocolate and life comes through as soon as you enter the shop, where he will guide you through his inventive flavors, from white chocolate hibiscus to three chile with lime-orange essence.

GOOD TO KNOW Shugarman's offers dairy-free and vegan options. *2842 State Road 14. (505) 474–9041.*

Albuquerque

The Candy Lady of Old Town

The AMC TV series *Breaking Bad* and its prequel *Better Call Saul* put Albuquerque on the map. It also put the Candy Lady, aka Debbie Ball, and her sweets shop in Old Town Albuquerque in a bizarre spotlight. The show was shot in various locations around Albuquerque, and the *Breaking Bad* props department asked Ball, who makes her own flavored rock candy, to create a substance that resembled the show's signature blue meth. She decided to sell the blue rock candy to fans of the show, and, not surprisingly, it's been a hit ever since. She also makes nut clusters, fudge, toffees, truffles, and other treats, and, yes, she *is* the danger.

GOOD TO KNOW The Candy Lady is well-known for its X-rated product line, a popular stop for those planning bachelorette parties. *424 San Felipe Street NW. (505) 243–6239; thecandylady.com.*

Eldora Craft Chocolate

It's great to see a dream come true, especially when it involves chocolate. Retired Merrill Lynch consultant Steve Prickett built this little half-acre oasis with his wife, Andrea, near Los Ranchos de Albuquerque as a "destination for chocolate lovers." He gets his cacao beans from several sustainable and ethical sources and transforms the beans into bars and bonbons. Prickett is one of only a handful of bean-to-bar chocolate makers in New Mexico, so this is a special place to soak up some knowledge and witness this chocolate maker's dedication to the craft. Eldora offers tours and tasting sessions so that chocolate lovers can determine whether they prefer the fruit-forward flavors of a Madagascar bar or the more earthy essence of Mexican beans. Prickett's goal "is to figure out what's in the bean and how to tease it out." Either way, your taste buds are going to thank you.

GOOD TO KNOW Many of the products here are vegan friendly. *8114 Edith Boulevard NE. (505) 433–4076; eldorachocolate .com.*

Golden Crown Panaderia

Come for the coffee milkshake; stay for the empanadas. And the cookies. And the breads. And the pizzas. This father–son outfit has all the ingredients of a traditional New Mexico bakery, from its quaint little adobe that houses a handful of tables to the slightly bigger kitchen where the popular (and I would argue magical) green chile bread and dozens of other delights are mixed, kneaded, rolled, stuffed, and baked. The coffee milkshake calls to me with its thick vanilla ice cream base, two espresso shots, and injection of dark chocolate (topped with whipped cream, of course). The blueberry empanada is another favorite—the crust melts away, giving your mouth plenty of space to enjoy the fruit filling. And while I'm usually a traditionalist, I

favor the cappuccino-flavored biscochitos. Locals also know to come here around Thanksgiving for a loaf of the bakery's turkey-shaped bread, one of owner-patriarch Pratt Morales's many works of art.

GOOD TO KNOW Enjoy a New Mexico craft beer as well as a wine selection with your pizza and breads here. *1103 Mountain Road NW. (505) 243–2424; goldencrown.biz.*

Pop Fizz

I'm pretty sure there's nothing more satisfying on a hot New Mexico summer afternoon than a paleta in the park. A paleta is a magical fruit-centric popsicle from Mexico that comes in a rainbow of colors and flavors. Mango? Chile-lime dipped in chile powder? Mexican chocolate? Avocado? Yes to all. For old-fashioned chocolate ice cream fans, Pop Fizz's chocolate taco scratches that itch with its thick slab of ice cream folded inside a waffle cone that is then coated in chocolate and frozen to the perfect texture. A precaution: If it's a typical Albuquerque summer day, eat it quickly or you'll need lots of napkins.

GOOD TO KNOW Check out some of the alcohol-infused treats here, such as the paleta mimosa (adults only). *Albuquerque: 530 Bridge Blvd. SW. Los Ranchos de Albuquerque: 6770 Fourth Street NW. (505) 508–1082; popfizzabq.com.*

Rebel Donut

The fancy doughnut craze might've come and gone, but the few who knew how to maintain the quality and develop a loyal following still remain. This shop, which has been turning out holey treats since 2012,

Find cool treats with Mexican and New Mexican twists at Pop Fizz, an Albuquerque paleta bar.

now has two locations and a display case that, at times, looks more like a little art gallery than a doughnut tray. Is it May 4 (May the Fourth)? Then you'll want to swing by for an array of *Star Wars*–themed doughnuts glazed to look like C-3PO and Yoda. Is it Balloon Fiesta season? Oh, yes, the shop has balloon-shaped yeasty treats. Other holidays bring a cornucopia of flavors and shapes, although the shop doesn't neglect the classics, such as the simple raised glazed or the chocolate-topped chocolate cake. In the fancy category, you don't want to miss the chocolate cake doughnut dipped in fudge icing and topped with red chile powder and bacon. If you like a little more breakfast heft, the apple and green chile fritter is out of this world.

GOOD TO KNOW Good news for those stuck at the office: Rebel also delivers. *2435 Wyoming Boulevard NE; (505) 293–0553. 9311 Coors Boulevard NW, Suite QA; (505) 898–3090. rebeldonut.com.*

Pie Town

Pie-O-Neer Pies

Many of New Mexico's towns were founded by enterprising prospectors, who staked claims and tried to scratch a living out of the hardscrabble rocks. One such soul, Clyde Norman, staked a claim here in the 1920s and also opened a mercantile, where he liked to bake pies. The sweets turned out to be more sustainable and people-pleasing than mining, and pie emerged as one of the best commodities. The main game in this sleepy little town on the Continental Divide National Scenic Trail has been the Pie-O-Neer, but it is currently for sale. We crustifarians are hopeful that new owners will continue the tradition of serving pie and hospitality in this storied stretch of New Mexico desert.

GOOD TO KNOW Currently closed but hoping pies will spring forth again soon. Get updates at facebook.com/pieoneer. *5613 U.S. Highway 60. (575) 772–2711; pieoneer.com.*

Hatch

Sparky's Burgers, BBQ, and Espresso

Most of us are so enamored by the green chile cheeseburgers that it's easy to forget that there's more here than just meat. Sparky's also offers ice cream and espresso, the latter being the passion of Josie Nunn, who owns the restaurant with her husband, Teako. Let's start with the treats, which will not only satisfy your sweet tooth but also remind you that you're in chile country. Folks rave about the chile mango shake, which infuses red chile heat into vanilla soft serve and mixes it with tropical fruit and chocolate syrup. The fresh-squeezed lemonades come sassy (with red chile and strawberry) or with green chile, of course.

Put out the chile fire with a frozen treat at Sparky's Burgers, BBQ, and Espresso in Hatch.

A Word about Fry Bread

Not all fry bread is created equal. Each of the nineteen recognized pueblos and three reservations in New Mexico has its own slight twist or version, which, when made just right, becomes a bubbly piece of fried heaven sprinkled with powdered sugar or drizzled with honey. While it's become a staple of many Native American communities and is readily offered for sale to tourists, this seemingly innocuous food has a complicated history. About 150 years ago, when large groups of Native peoples were forced from their lands in the Southwest to endure long marches, they were denied access to their usual foods. To survive on the meager provisions provided by the US government, they used the flour, processed sugar, and lard to create a bread that would sustain them. While buying fry bread at the pueblos can be mutually beneficial, there are additional ways to experience Native foods, which tend to be more about bison, mutton, beans, squash, and foraged plants and herbs, and less about sweets.

Patronizing Native-owned eateries and businesses benefits the people and their pueblos says Andi Murphy, who is Diné and grew up on the Crownpoint Reservation, about sixty miles northeast of Gallup. A journalist, an associate producer of a Native American call-in radio show, a dedicated foodie, and the creator of her own award-winning *Toasted Sister* podcast, Murphy notes that while finding Native foods isn't easy, there are places that are worth a deeper dive. "New Mexico food wouldn't be New Mexico food if it weren't for indigenous people," she says.

Ray Naranjo, a member of Santa Clara Pueblo and the chef at Pueblo Harvest Café (soon to be renamed Indian Pueblo Kitchen) at the Indian Pueblo Cultural Center in Albuquerque, has created a menu that is approachable but also reflects Pueblo culture and includes pre-contact elements. "The focus is modern Native cuisine," he says, but it incorporates ingredients such as blue corn from Santa Ana Pueblo and three types of beans—black, pinto, and Anasazi—that traditionally are grown together. *indianpueblo.org.*

Or try the bread and other treats from Grandma Jo's Bakery at Casa Blanca on I-40, near the turnoff to Acoma Pueblo. At powwows and pueblo feast days, you'll find fry bread, Pueblo breads, and other foods to sample. Murphy also recommends a trip to the Gallup Ninth Street Flea Market, where you can find kneel-down bread—a tamale pudding made from milky and sweet young corn, which is mushed, wrapped into a corn husk, and buried under a fire to bake. Market vendors also sell Navajo tea, mutton stew, various types of breads, and other intriguing foods and desert herbs. *gallup9th.com.*

If you want zippy instead of spicy with your creamy treat, try the Mudball, an espresso jazzed up with vanilla soft serve and chocolate syrup. (Read more in the "Green Chile Cheeseburger" chapter.)

GOOD TO KNOW This place is swinging, especially during chile harvest season and on weekends, when live bands play. Get there early or try to hold off till after the lunch rush. *115 Franklin Street. (575) 267-4222; sparkysburgers.com.*

Las Cruces

Caliche's Frozen Custard

This outdoor treat spot has become a social center for locals during the summer, when everyone comes after dinner with their dogs and kids, orders a cool treat, and enjoys a warm New Mexico sunset. The menu here is vast, with most of it centering around frozen custard, which is made with cream, sugar, and egg yolks, making for a richer, denser treat than ice cream. Numerous flavor combinations of shakes, massive banana splits, sundaes, and scoops make it hard to choose; toppings range from kiwi to pineapple, from cookie dough to green chile, creating a real dessert quandary. When the place opened in 1996 as Scoopy's, locals were a little slow to warm to the concept of frozen custard. But now with two Las Cruces locations and one in Alamogordo, it's obviously a hit.

GOOD TO KNOW Doggies love this place—they get a free "poochie cone" with a purchase when they visit with their humans. (Dogs must be leashed while enjoying their custard.) *Las Cruces: 590 S. Valley Drive; (575) 647–5066. 131 S. Roadrunner Parkway; (575) 521–1161. Alamogordo: 2251 N. White Sands Blvd.; (575) 439–1000. caliches.com.*

Legacy Pecans, Mesilla

The Mesilla Valley is pecan country, and bags of them are readily available at grocery stores and farmers markets in the area. But for the sweet stuff, head to Legacy Pecans. This beautifully designed store on the Historic Mesilla Plaza is chockful of pecan products and treats. The shop is the brainchild of Heather Salopek, a fourth-generation member of the pecan royalty family of Salopeks, who've been growing nuts in this valley since 1923. At this chic little shop you can pick up pecan butter, pecan syrup, pralines, gift packs, and just plain ol' pecans. I

Sopaipillas are de rigueur at most New Mexican food restaurants, including Si Señor in Las Cruces.

would highly recommend that you not leave this shop without a can of pecan-dusted brittle.

GOOD TO KNOW Closed on Tuesdays. *2355 Calle de Guadalupe. (575) 524–1362; legacypecans.com.*

Si Señor Restaurant

Guess what, kids? Dessert is a given at this popular locals' spot. A basket of golden pillows of fried dough comes standard with your meal. The only choice you have to make is whether to go the traditional plain route or try them dusted with cinnamon and sugar. Request to have them brought at the end of your meal, so they're still crisp and warm when you're ready for dessert. Then bite off a tip of the corner, let out some steam, and fill the pocket with a bit of honey (or sopaipilla syrup, as we say here). Rotate the honey inside as you chew. If you work it just right, the honey will fill the fourth corner, making the last bite the best thing on earth.

GOOD TO KNOW A stop at Si Señor Express at 500 S. Solano Drive can shorten the wait times between sopaipillas and your stomach. *1551 E. Amador Avenue. (575) 527–0817; sisenor.com.*

Hillsboro

Hillsboro General Store Café

Do yourself a favor and take a side trip to the Hillsboro General Store for a slice of its bumbleberry pie. Bumbleberry isn't a berry but rather a mishmash of several fruits, including raspberry, rhubarb (is that a fruit?), blueberry, blackberry—well, you get

Stop by Hillsboro General Store Café for a slice of bumbleberry pie à la mode.

A Word about Biscochitos

Yes, this is New Mexico's official state cookie. But why do we offer such high praise for a simple cookie flavored with what some would argue are polarizing spices (anise seeds, I'm talking to you)? For me, it was all about the Saturday mornings of my youth spent at the Las Cruces Farmers and Crafts Market. My sister sold her artwork there, so after she was set up, I'd start cruising for treats. I almost always stopped at Mrs. Ochoa's booth, which, in addition to offering a range of herbal remedies and spices, sold the best biscochos (as we call them down south) on the downtown mall (and beyond). They were lardy and flaky, on the thicker side, and shaped like elongated diamonds. So biscochitos are part of a New Mexican childhood, no matter which part of the state you grew up in (or what you call them). As with all New Mexican delicacies, each

baker brings his or her own flavors, shapes, and thicknesses. At the farmers market, the Osito's Biscochitos cart is a popular spot to restock your supply (the raspberry habanero are my fave), albeit these cookies are small (which means more cinnamon sugar per bite). Up north, the Celina's Biscochitos version is ubiquitous. This cookie is scalloped on the edges and on the thinner side, which gives it a crispier texture. The Lovin Oven in Española gets high marks for its biscochitos and also produces a killer cinnamon roll. So here's my advice: If you're at a bakery, a store, a restaurant, a gift shop, or a market in New Mexico that sells a biscochito you haven't tried, pick up a bag. It's never going to rise to the level of Mrs. Ochoa's, but you will have your own memory.

the picture. The result is a warm, deep purple, slightly tart filling wrapped in a flaky crust that you'd swear your grandma made, if your grandma was the baking type. A scoop of vanilla ice cream gives it just the right balance. They'll ring up your bill on the ornate cash register, an original from the 1890s, when this building was a mercantile serving the residents of this historic mining town. (Read more in the "Green Chile Cheeseburger" chapter.)

GOOD TO KNOW After pie, wander over to the Black Range Museum, a colorful and rich repository of local history. *10697 State Road 152. (575) 895–5306; facebook.com /hillsborogeneralstorecafe.*

Alamogordo

McGinn's Pistachioland

This is more than just a place to take your photo with the world's largest pistachio. Step away from the nut and into the sprawling log cabin–style general store and take your pick from more than a dozen flavors of pistachios dusted with red and green chile, habanero lime, barbecue, and bacon ranch seasonings, among others (or just roasted with salt). Enjoy some wine, sample the nuts at the pistachio bar, visit the ice cream parlor for a scoop of pistachio ice cream, and then jump on the lime green trolley for a tour of the orchards and a lesson in local pistachio history and trivia. (Did you know the nuts fall off the tree half open, just like they come in the bag?) Finish up by browsing all the gourmet food products in the gift store (including a wide array of pistachio candy made in-house), and by all means, don't leave without a "Going Nuts" T-shirt. (Read more in the wine and spirits chapter.)

GOOD TO KNOW The orchard tours are well worth the $2 charge. *7320 US 54/70 North. (575) 437–0602; pistachioland.com.*

A giant nut marks the spot to find pistachios made into treats of every flavor at McGinn's Pistachioland in Alamogordo.

Cloudcroft

Burro Street Bakery, KennaBelle's Kreations Bakery, Eight the Cake

Why is pie so much better at higher elevations? Maybe it's because it serves as the perfect reward for a day of hiking the web of trails winding through the Lincoln National Forest, which surrounds this quaint mountain village of fewer than seven hundred people. Or maybe it's just that skilled pie makers prefer thinner air. The Burro Street boardwalk, which is only a few blocks long, somehow manages to support three worth-the-drive bakeries: KennaBelle's Kreations, the Burro Street Bakery, and Eight the Cake. It's cruel to force people to choose between the green chile bacon rolls and the cinnamon rolls heaped with pecans at Kenna-Belle's, the Berries of the Forest and the caramel apple walnut pies at Burro Street, and the artistic cupcakes and pies stuffed with locally grown cherries, apples, and other fruits at Eight the Cake. One option? Sample whatever grabs your eye and then meander among the shops and galleries along Burro Avenue.

GOOD TO KNOW The three shops are all within a few hundred feet of each other, so you can easily make an afternoon out of bakery hopping. *Burro Street Bakery: 505 Burro Avenue, Suite 106. (575) 682–2777. KennaBelle's Kreations: 308 Burro Avenue. (575) 682–2712. Eight the Cake: 506A Burro Avenue. (575) 682–3088; eightthecakellc.com.*

Ruidoso

Sacred Grounds Coffee and Tea House

Live music. Comfy couches. House-baked pastries and an array of quiches. A well-stocked gift shop. Coffee that'll stand up to a cool Ruidoso morning. Oh, and local booze and beer. What started as a humble coffee and tea house in 2010 has evolved to fill a sprawling woodsy cabin overlooking the Rio Ruidoso and offering food, beverages to fill all vessels, and entertainment. In the late afternoon or evening, my favorite spot is on the couch near the back deck, where I can order a Moscow Mule made from local Glencoe Distillery vodka and relax to the sounds of a crackling fire and gurgling river. On my way out, I usually

grab a scone and a bag of fresh-roasted Sacred Grounds whole bean coffee as a reminder that it's important to stop, sip good coffee, and enjoy the scenery. (Read more in the wine and spirits chapter.)

GOOD TO KNOW You can enjoy live music on most weekends. *2704 Sudderth Drive. (575) 257–2273; sacredgrounds-coffee-and-tea-house.com.*

Tina's Café

What happens when you chop up bacon, mix it with a sugar glaze, and pour that over a mandala of dough? You get the famed Pig Candy Cinnamon Roll, which has been feeding hungry hikers and skiers for the past decade. Owner Tina Greene knows her way around a pie crust too, and folks (okay, me) have been known to drive for miles for her baked-from-scratch red chile pecan, green chile apple, and coconut cream pies.

GOOD TO KNOW During the summer, check out the Sinatra-style live music on the patio. *2825 Sudderth Drive. (575) 257–8930.*

Lovington

Lazy 6

"Believe me, you have to try this chocolate cake." So said my brother-in-law, John, a Lovington newspaper publisher who seems to thrive on an endless supply of energy and enthusiasm—for everything. Whether he's talking up his favorite travel coffee mug or his top pick for enchiladas (see his recommendation for Club Gas in the "Green and Red" chapter), the intensity is always high. So I was skeptical of his chocolate cake recommendation, especially since I'd already filled up on a pile of steak fingers as big as my head here. (They were great, especially dipped in the house-made ranch dressing.) But even John's unbridled enthusiasm didn't do the cake justice. This is a

The chocolate cake at Lazy 6 in Lovington is basic and unfettered by fancy frosting, but it is the stuff of dreams.

Blue House Bakery and Café in Carlsbad is the place to stop for pastries and coffee drinks.

special one, especially for weird cake eaters such as myself, who often scrape off sugary globs of frosting in favor of finding a flavorful cake. This version is a basic sheet cake, with no fancy fillings but just a pure layer of perfectly satisfying, rich cake. On top is a paper-thin layer of sugar glaze, which seeps into the cake, creating a filmy, sugary crust that makes the cake even more moist and chocolatey. Throw a scoop of homemade ice cream on top and you've got one of the best diner desserts in New Mexico.

GOOD TO KNOW Cash only. Usually open only for lunch, and hours are limited and can fluctuate, so call ahead. *102 S. First Street A. (575) 396–5066.*

Carlsbad

Blue House Bakery and Café

Coffee cake, cheesecake, cinnamon rolls, sticky buns: Where to start? Perhaps it's

with a powdered sugar–dusted chocolate croissant, one of the standouts on the menu. (And the plain croissants are buttery and fluffy and leave just the right amount of flakes on the front of your shirt.) The coffee and coffee-flavored drinks get high marks here too, especially for those looking for a jolt to begin a hike through Carlsbad Caverns National Park. If you decide to sit and enjoy your pastry, you'll find an ample porch with outdoor tables under big shade trees. Or sit inside the house-turned-café, which, with its cozy nooks and wood floors, feels like an eatery you'd find in a small California mountain town.

GOOD TO KNOW Open 6 a.m. to noon; closed Sundays. *609 N. Canyon Street. (575) 628–0555.*

Take Five: Where to Brake for Coffee Breaks

Coffeehouses brewed mostly in obscurity until you-know-who showed up and made us crave lattes and working on our computers in public spaces. We are now entering the third wave of this craze, which has helped elevate both the beans and the spaces. The following are New Mexico's top spots to simultaneously chill and over-caffeinate.

1. **TAOS** Mountain towns love their coffees, and Taos is no exception. Drop in at Elevation Coffee, where the baristas take their time to craft the perfect beverage for you and, in the process, create works of art in the foam. Look for the big red tilted coffee cup outside. *elevationcoffeeshoppe.com.*

2. **SANTA FE** The City Different is buzzing with coffee hangouts. My top pick? Iconik Coffee Roasters, which has three locations. The one near the plaza on Galisteo Street is tucked into the charming Collected Works Bookstore, but the Guadalupe Street location has the creative vibe many of us seek. And the gluten-free muffins are delicious and moist, and I don't like gluten-free anything. *iconikcoffee.com.*

3. **ALBUQUERQUE** It's no surprise that the coffee craze has done well in our state's biggest city. Bean snobs congregate at Cutbow Coffee Roastery near Old Town, which roasts on-site and offers a curated selection of coffees that you can sample by the flight. *cutbowcoffee.com.* If you're craving something sweet, hit up New Mexico Piñon Coffee (which has two cafés in Albuquerque and one in Rio Rancho). This ubiquitous coffee company sells beans everywhere and also has a popular storefront, where the extensive menu of hot, cold, and blended coffee drinks capitalizes on New Mexico flavors (such as pecan, pistachio, and biscochito). *pinoncoffeehouse.com.*

4. **SOCORRO** That long drive between Las Cruces and Albuquerque requires a coffee stop in Socorro, and M Mountain Coffee House fits the bill. Just look for the coffee mural on the side of the building near downtown. The breakfast sandwiches are delicious and filling too. *(575) 838-0809.*

5. **LAS CRUCES** As an early adopter of the coffee house trend (this is a college town, after all), Las Cruces has nurtured its homey little roasting houses. It's tough to pick a favorite. I like the snacks (artisanal ice cream!) and the atmosphere at Beck's Roasting House and Creamery, but the Bean Bakery Café near Mesilla holds a big place in my heart for always being there when I needed an afternoon cappuccino for studying or rejuvenating. *beckscoffeelc.com; facebook.com/bean cafemesilla.*

New Mexico is riding the third wave of the coffee craze.

10 Let's Go Eat
Foodie Jaunts and Quick Escapes

Food experiences happen all over the state, in a variety of ways. This chapter offers a range of excursions, outings, explorations, and getaways that include tasty adventures.

Santa Fe / Taos Area

Day Trips

TAOS | WILD EARTH LLAMA ADVENTURES

Want to go on a picnic but don't want the hassle of carrying food into the forest? Or perhaps you're looking for a fresh-faced hiking companion who won't complain about holding your heavy backpack? Wild Earth Llama Adventures offers a Take a Llama to Lunch Wilderness hike, a highly motivating way to get out into nature and make a cool new friend. The llamas do the heavy lifting, and along with experienced guides, you traverse a series of trails through either the Rio Grande Gorge or the Sangre de Cristo Mountains to a designated spot, where you chow down on a gourmet spread. *(800) 758–5262; llamaadventures .com.*

CHIMAYÓ

This picturesque community is known for producing heirloom chile that is as hot as the Hatch varieties but grown in smaller quantities. You can buy the pods and powders at gift shops and galleries throughout this tight-knit, dirt-road town. A tour here should also include a stop at the Santuario de Chimayó, a historic church that draws pilgrimages of thousands of Catholics each spring. A room at the back of the church is said to contain holy dirt that, according to testimonies from pilgrims dating back to the early 1800s, has physical and spiritual healing properties. (Visitors are welcome to collect a small bag of dirt.) Stop for lunch or dinner (or a margarita) at Rancho de Chimayó, a restaurant, inn, and gift shop that's been serving hungry visitors for more than five decades. In 2016 the restaurant received a James Beard Foundation America's Classics Award. *(505) 351–4444; rancho dechimayo.com.*

ABIQUIÚ

This is Georgia O'Keeffe country, and a look at its dramatic sandstone cliffs and volcanic formations explains why the artist was so deeply attracted to it. The best way to get to know O'Keeffe is by taking the guided tour of her Abiquiú home and studio. She was drawn to a simple life and an uncluttered aesthetic. She loved her garden and using its fruits in her utilitarian kitchen, which is a popular stop on the tour. She also spent time at a home at nearby Ghost Ranch, which today offers retreats, classes, tours of O'Keeffe sites, museums, and outdoor activities. *O'Keeffe Museum: (505) 946–1000; okeeffemuseum .org. Ghost Ranch: (505) 685–1000; ghostranch.org.*

SANTA FE | WANDER NEW MEXICO

One of the best ways to get to know a town is by taking a food tour with a local expert.

Make food discoveries, learn some history, try some nibbles and drinks, and get to know other foodies on these culinary tours, which wander through various Santa Fe and Albuquerque neighborhoods. Tours are typically two to four hours, and you'll be stuffed full of both food and knowledge. *(505) 395–0552; wandernewmexico.com.*

SANTA FE | GREEN CHILE CHEESEBURGER SMACKDOWN

In September, *Edible New Mexico* sponsors one of the state's most prestigious annual burger battles. Chefs from all corners of the state bring their most bodacious burger recipes to go bun to bun for bragging rights. An expert panel chooses a Reigning Chomp, while the common folks vote to select the People's Choice. But really, everyone wins, since participants get to test out their best burger game, and tasters get to sample a range of burgers. *ediblesmackdown.com.*

SANTA FE SCHOOL OF COOKING

Learn to make contemporary and traditional Mexican, New Mexican, and Native dishes from experts in these cuisines at this Santa Fe institution. It has been a hot spot for southwestern cooking since it opened in 1989. The school offers hands-on and demonstration classes on a variety of cooking-related topics as well as chef-led walking tours to various Santa Fe restaurants and wine-tasting rooms. The gift shop is stocked with an array of kitchen- and food-related items. *(505) 983–4511; santafeschoolofcooking.com.*

Quick Escapes

LAS VEGAS

With nearly one thousand buildings on the National Register of Historic Places, you can't toss a pebble around here without hitting a significant site. Fortunately for visitors, many of these spots are being transformed for modern use. Case in point: the Castaneda Hotel, a former Harvey House rescued from near ruin to resume its life as a hotel. Its historic charm intact, it also offers such modern amenities as a popular bar serving craft cocktails (see page 89) and a killer green chile cheeseburger (see page 27). *(505) 434–1005; kinlvnm.com.* While you're in town, opt for one of Southwest Detours' history tours for a glimpse inside some of Las Vegas's cool buildings and a dose of Wild West history. *(505) 459–6987; southwestdetours.com.*

CHAMA

The romance of train travel is alive and well aboard the Cumbres & Toltec Scenic Railroad, which offers excursions from Antonito, Colorado, to scenic Chama

Chile is worshipped in the quaint town of Chimayó, where local farmers grow their own heirloom variety.

through the tippy-top of New Mexico. The train chugs along some rugged terrain, across wildflower fields, over picturesque trestles, and through dramatic tunnels carved through rocky hillsides. The train makes a stop for lunch in Osier, Colorado, or riders can opt for the prime rib offered on one of the sunset dinner trains. *(888) 286–2737; cumbrestoltec.com.*

OJO CALIENTE MINERAL SPRINGS RESORT AND SPA

These healing waters have been soothing muscles and minds for hundreds of years. Available massages and beauty treatments include everything from an East Indian head massage to a Native American blue corn and prickly pear salt scrub (sounds delicious). The accommodations have private soaking tubs and kiva fireplaces, among other amenities. Another top reason to visit this secluded oasis is the Artesian Restaurant, which features an innovative farm-to-table menu that ranges from fresh twists on New Mexico classics such as chiles rellenos to comfort dishes like chicken pot pie. Ojo's two-acre farm provides fresh produce for a dedicated salad menu. *(888) 939–0007; ojospa.com.*

Albuquerque Area

Day Trips

BALLOONING

The Albuquerque International Balloon Fiesta is a nine-day event held annually in early October, and the sight of balloons glowing, lifting off, and filling the sky with colorful shapes and designs never gets tiresome. Balloon Fiesta days start well before dawn, so begin by buying a breakfast burrito from one of the many vendors at Balloon Fiesta Park. Then spread out a blanket,

The elegant Ten 3 restaurant atop the Sandia Peak Tramway serves beautiful cocktails along with breathtaking views.

sit back, and watch the show. The mass ascension, with balloons taking off all around you, is breathtaking. *balloonfiesta .com.* If you want to soar instead of watch, Albuquerque-area companies offer hot air balloon excursions throughout the year. Depending on wind patterns, these rides might include a touch-and-go on the Río Grande. They traditionally end with a champagne toast (typically with New Mexico's own Gruet bubbly; see page 91).

FOODIE BIKE TOURS

Sure, Routes Bicycle Tours offers scenic treks on the bosque trails alongside the Río Grande. But the company also offers guided winery and brewery treks, as well as New Mexico chile tours, with six stops at places serving chile in a variety of forms. Santa Fe restaurant and brewery bike tours are available too. *(505) 933–5667; routes rentals.com.*

SANDIA PEAK TRAMWAY

The cuisine, the cocktails, and the views are highfalutin at Ten 3, the fine-dining restaurant that sits at an elevation of 10,300 feet atop Sandia Peak. The trip to and from the top takes place on the Sandia Peak Tramway. The breathtaking fifteen-minute gondola ride up the side of the Sandias reveals expansive views of Albuquerque and points beyond. You don't have to dine at the restaurant. You can just grab a cocktail at the bar or opt for a hike. (There's a ski hill up here too.) Just remember that this is high elevation and pace yourself. *Ten 3: (505) 764–8363; ten3tram.com. Sandia Peak Tramway: (505) 856–7325; sandiapeak.com.*

SAWMILL MARKET

A colorful collection of eateries, shops, and hangout spots is the hallmark of this aesthetically pleasing food hall, which became Albuquerque's first such place when it opened in early 2019. The space is the brainchild of the developers of Heritage Hotels, a regional chain that incorporates local culture into its properties. They transformed this former warehouse into a lively open space where foodies can grab coffee, pizza, fresh bread, and local craft beer, and shop for such artisanal goodies as candles, chocolate, olive oil, and succulents. *sawmill market.com.*

Quick Escapes

HYATT REGENCY TAMAYA RESORT AND SPA, SANTA ANA PUEBLO

Even Albuquerque locals vacation at this 550-acre destination resort with a golf course, casino, spa, horseback riding, and cultural activities led by members of Santa Ana Pueblo, which owns the property. The Corn Maiden fine-dining restaurant features such Pueblo-inspired dishes as a native beef rib eye served with yucca frites. *(505) 867–1234; hyatt.com.*

GALLUP

Interstate 40 roughly parallels Route 66, taking travelers past the wide-open vistas and quirky small towns that help make the Mother Road such an adventure. Hopi and Zuni pueblos, as well as the Navajo Nation, sit all around Gallup, where a large portion of the population is Native American. The area is well-known for its trading posts, where Native artisans have traded wares and works for decades. Collectors and shoppers can buy rugs, jewelry, pottery, paintings, and other works created by local artists at such places as the Ellis Tanner Trading Company and Richardson's Trading Company. Downtown, check out the City Electric Shoe Shop, which makes and sells moccasins and other leather goods. On Saturdays, the Gallup Ninth Street Flea Market fills up with hundreds of vendors selling horno-baked bread, mutton stew, fry bread, and other dishes, as well as traditional herbs and plenty of art. *(505) 399–2166; gallup9th.com.*

Las Cruces Area

Day Trips

LAS CRUCES | D. H. LESCOMBES WINE TOUR

Let someone else do the driving while you do the sipping during a guided tour of this well-established vineyard. Begin with lunch at Lescombes Bistro in Las Cruces and then take a 120-mile drive to the 180-acre vineyard near Lordsburg. After that, it's off to Deming for tours of the winery and a six-barrel VIP wine tasting (see page 96). *(575) 524–2408; lescombeswinery.com.*

DOWNTOWN LAS CRUCES AND BEYOND

Begin Saturday morning at the Farmers and Crafts Market of Las Cruces, where you can stock up on biscochos (see page 109), fresh sourdough loaves, handmade crafts, local art, and fresh produce. *(575) 201–3853; farmersandcraftsmarketoflascruces.com.* While you're at the market, stop in Organ Mountain Outfitters for T-shirts, hats, hoodies, and other gear that will inspire you to explore this town's biggest natural landmark: the Organ Mountains. *(575) 800–4895; organmountainoutfitters.com.* Expanded and named the Organ Mountains-Desert Peaks National Monument by presidential proclamation in 2014, this area is rife with hiking trails and dramatic views. On the west side of the Organs, you can access the Dripping Springs Natural Area, which has an easy trail to scenic picnic tables and a series of springs running from the rock walls of the mountains. *(575) 525–4300; blm.gov/visit/omdp.*

ARDOVINO'S DESERT CROSSING, SUNLAND PARK

Carved into a sliver of New Mexico land that divides Texas and Mexico sits a hidden culinary gem. It started as a hangout in the 1940s, and a new generation of the Ardovino family has renovated the property and resurrected its spirit, enhancing it with some of the best farm-to-table, Italian-influenced dishes in the state. Guests drive from Las Cruces and El Paso to experience such worth-the-trek dishes as lamb pappardelle (with house-made pasta) and a Chimayó red chile–rubbed New York strip. There's also a Saturday morning farmers market offering produce from regional growers, locally raised meat, fresh-baked goods, coffee served from an Airstream trailer, and even a yoga class (with mimosas). For those who want to dine and stay, the property recently opened three renovated vintage travel trailers, perched atop the hardscrabble desert overlooking two countries and three states. *(575) 589–0653; ardovinos.com.*

COLUMBUS AND PALOMAS, MEXICO

Grab your passport for a trip across the remote border crossing at Columbus to venture over to Palomas, Mexico, and The Pink Store. Shoppers receive a free margarita to sip as they browse the hand-carved furniture, pottery, and other made-in-Mexico goodies. (A restaurant here serves Mexican food with beers and margaritas.) *(575) 545–5206; thepinkstoremexico.com.* Hop back over to the US side at Columbus to explore Pancho Villa State Park (named for the Mexican Revolution military leader who led an attack on US soil in 1916) and Rockhound State Park, where visitors are allowed to hunt for and collect geodes and other geologic treasures. *emnrd.state.nm.us.*

Quick Escapes

SILVER CITY

Start the day by grabbing pastries and sandwiches at Diane's Bakery and Deli (see page 13). Then head for Gila Cliff Dwellings National Monument, about forty-five miles north of Silver City. The park preserves the sites of the Mogollon peoples who lived here between 1270 and 1300. The surrounding Gila National Forest, which became the first national wilderness in the United States when it was established in 1924, contains hundreds of miles of hiking trails as well as an abundance of campgrounds. A perfect top-off to a day of hiking and exploring is a visit to the small but mighty La Esperanza Vineyard and Winery (see page 95), a family-owned operation set on a beautiful slice of country just south of Gila National Forest. Nearby in hilly Hillsboro,

Cloudcroft visitors stop for apple-flavored treats, T-shirts, and other local goodies at this venerable roadside store.

wine-tasting and mining history merge at the quaint Black Range Winery (see page 93), where you can sip wines and New Mexico craft beers and then enjoy a piece of pie at the Hillsboro General Store (see page 109), a building that dates back to the 1880s.

RUIDOSO

If you're ready to horse around, this is the place to do it. Start with a morning horseback ride at one of several stables in and around Ruidoso and then catch an afternoon race or two at Ruidoso Downs (May through Labor Day). *(575) 378-4431; raceruidoso.com.* End the day with a chuck-wagon dinner at the Flying J, a western-themed attraction with staged gunfights and live music (see page 57). *(575) 336-4330; flyingjranch.com.* Spend the night at the Inn of the Mountain Gods, a luxury resort owned by the Mescalero Apache Tribe that features a zipline, a golf course, a nearby ski resort, fine dining at Wendell's

Steak and Seafood, and the Broken Arrow Taphouse, serving several New Mexico beers. *(800) 545-9011; innofthemountain-gods.com.* Or spend a day playing on the glistening gypsum dunes at White Sands National Park, which got an upgrade from national monument to become our newest national park in 2019. *(575) 479-6124; nps. gov/whsa/index.htm.* Nearby is Alamogordo, where you can take a selfie with the world's largest pistachio statue at Pistachioland (see page 96). *(800) 368-3081; pistachioland.com.* Up US 82 just west of Cloudcroft, drop by the Old Apple Barn, where the Barn Bistro serves a tasty smoked elk sausage in addition to a well-curated selection of pies and other treats. *(575) 682-2276; oldapple barn.com.* Spend the night at the venerable Lodge Resort and Spa at Cloudcroft, a former playground for such celebrities as Judy Garland and Clark Gable. It also serves fine dining at Rebecca's, a restaurant beloved by locals and haunted by its namesake ghost. *(800) 395-6343; thelodgeresort.com.*

11 The List
Twenty-Five Dishes to Drive For

The following is a highly subjective list of menu items from restaurants throughout New Mexico that are worth the drive. This list is ever-evolving, so stay tuned at *newmexicofoodtrails.com*.

1. Chocolate Mousse, Chokolá Bean to Bar, Taos, (575) 779-6163 (see page 100)

2. Chicken Wings with Ken'z Specialty Dipping Sauce, Blue Heron Brewing Company/Ken'z Cuisine, Española, (505) 747-4506 (see page 80)

3. Haystax House-Cut Fries, Counter Culture, Santa Fe, (505) 995-1105

4. Banana Ice Cream, Shake Foundation, Santa Fe, (505) 988-8992 (see page 104)

5. House-Made Potato Chips, Santa Fe Bite, Santa Fe, (505) 428-0328 (see page 27)

6. Roast Chicken, Green Chile, Toasted Piñons, Blue Corn Crust Pizza, Draft Station, Santa Fe, (505) 983-6443

7. Posole, The Shed, Santa Fe, (505) 982-9030 (see page 49)

8. Breakfast Taco, The Skillet, Las Vegas, (505) 563-0477

9. Hatch Green Chile Basket, Mine Shaft Tavern, Madrid, (505) 473-0743

10. The Swirl, Tomasita's, Santa Fe and Albuquerque, (505) 983-5721 (see page 66)

The chocolate mousse is worth the drive to Chokolá Bean to Bar in Taos.

The wings pair nicely with the brews at Española's Blue Heron Brewing, but for aficionados, it's all about that dipping sauce.

The house-made potato chips at Santa Fe Bite have been known to cause more than a few feeding frenzies.

Those in need of a fast green chile cheeseburger fix can get it at Blake's Lotaburger, a popular New Mexico chain.

The breakfast taco at The Skillet in Las Vegas starts the morning right.

11. Balloon-Shaped Doughnuts, Rebel Donut, Albuquerque, (505) 293–0553 (see page 105)

12. Sweet Roll, Frontier Restaurant, Albuquerque, (505) 266–0550 (see page 17)

13. Red Chile Pork Tamales, El Modelo Mexican Foods, Albuquerque, (505) 242–1843

14. Spicy Blue Corn Waffle with Red or Green Chile, Tia Betty Blue's, Albuquerque, (505) 268–1955

15. Original New Mexico Green Chile Bread, Golden Crown Panaderia, Albuquerque, (505) 243–2424 (see page 105)

16. Red Chile Beef Bites, High Noon Restaurant and Saloon, Albuquerque, (505) 765–1455 (see page 52)

17. Flour Tortilla with Butter, Duran Central Pharmacy, Albuquerque, (505) 247–4141 (see page 10)

left Fresh-made tortillas and butter at Duran Central Pharmacy in Albuquerque. There's nothing finer.

right Folks drive from miles around for the rich onion soup at Adobe Deli in Deming.

18. Sopaipillas, Si Señor Restaurant, Las Cruces, (575) 527–0817 (see page 108)

19. Stuffed Green Chiles Fried in a Pecan Breading, Pecan Grill and Brewery, Las Cruces, (575) 521–1099

20. Adobe Deli Onion Soup, Adobe Deli, Deming, (575) 546–0361

21. Pistachio Chocolate Chip Cookies, McGinn's Pistachioland, Alamogordo, (800) 368–3081 (see page 110)

22. Sliced Brisket, Mad Jack's Mountaintop Barbecue, Cloudcroft, (575) 682–7577 (see page 37)

23. Chicken Fried Steak Fingers, Steak House Café, Tatum, (575) 398–9533

25. Lota Burger with Green Chile and Cheese, Blake's Lotaburger, Statewide

The line is always long at Mad Jack's Mountaintop Barbecue in Cloudcroft, but the brisket and other smoked meats are worth the wait.

12 The Guide
Trails by Region and Town

The following list is organized by region so that you can find your favorite places in the state. The cities and towns within each regional designation are arranged geographically, north to south and west to east.

Statewide

Eats
Blake's Lotaburger (pages 21 and 123)

Northern New Mexico

Farmington

EATS

3 Rivers Brewery Block (page 86)
AshKii's Navajo Grill (page 22)
The Chile Pod (page 45)

DRINKS

Bow and Arrow Brewing Company
  (page 77)
Three Rivers Eatery and Brewhouse
  (page 80)

Blanco

DRINK

Wines of the San Juan (page 87)

Chama

EATS

Cumbres & Toltec Scenic Railroad
  (page 115)

Find craft cocktails, good eats, and railroad history at the Legal Tender Saloon and Eating House in Lamy.

Abiquiú

EATS

Bodes General Store (page 23)
Ghost Ranch (page 114)

Española

EATS

Lovin Oven Bakery (page 109)
El Paragua (pages 45 and 53)
El Parasol (page 47)

DRINKS

Blue Heron Brewing Company
  (pages 80 and 121)

Pojoaque

EATS

El Parasol (page 47)

Chimayó

EATS

Rancho de Chimayó (page 114)

El Rito

EATS

El Farolito (page 53)

Ojo Caliente

EATS

Artesian Restaurant, Ojo Caliente Mineral
  Springs Resort and Spa (page 116)

Embudo

EATS

Sugar's BBQ (page 53)

DRINKS

Blue Heron Brewing Company (page 80)

Dixon

DRINKS

La Chiripada (page 86)
Vivác Winery (page 87)

Peñasco

EATS

Sugar Nymphs Bistro (page 102)

Taos

EATS

Chokolá Bean to Bar (pages 100 and 121)
Doc Martin's Restaurant, Taos Inn
 (page 47)
La Cueva Café (page 47)
Manzanita Market (page 7)
Michael's Kitchen Restaurant and Bakery
 (page 7)
Orlando's New Mexican Café
 (pages 47 and 100)
Taos Cow Ice Cream and Deli (page 102)
Wild Earth Llama Adventures (page 114)

DRINKS

Adobe Bar and Doc Martin's, Taos Inn
 (page 60)
Elevation Coffee (page 113)
La Chiripada (page 86)
Rolling Still Distillery (page 88)
Taos Mesa Brewing (page 75)

El Prado

DRINKS

Taos Mesa Brewing (page 75)

Red River

DRINKS

Noisy Water Winery (page 97)
Red River Brewing Company (page 76)

Eagle Nest

DRINKS

Comanche Creek Brewing Company
 (page 76)

Angel Fire

DRINKS

Enchanted Circle Brewing Company
 (page 76)

Santa Fe

EATS

Art of Chocolate, Cacao Santa Fe
 (page 102)
Cafe Pasqual's (page 48)
Chainé Cookie Shop (page 103)
Counter Culture (page 121)
Cowgirl Santa Fe (page 23)
Del Charro (page 25)
Draft Station (page 121)
El Chile Toreado (page 9)
El Farol (page 25)
El Parasol (page 47)
Five & Dime General Store
 (page 53)
Harry's Roadhouse (page 15)
Horseman's Haven Café (page 9)
Kakawa Chocolate House (page 103)
La Plazuela, La Fonda (page 10)
The Pantry (page 9)
Plaza Café (page 16)
The Original Realburger (page 26)
Santa Fe Bite (pages 27 and 121)
Santa Fe School of Cooking (page 115)
Shake Foundation (pages 27, 104,
 and 121)
The Shed (pages 49 and 121)
Tia Sophia's (page 49)

Las Vegas

Lamy

Madrid

Los Alamos

Jemez Springs

Gallup

Central New Mexico

Santa Ana Pueblo

Bernalillo

Rio Rancho

EATS

Twisters (page 12)

DRINKS

New Mexico Piñon Coffee Café (page 113)
Turtle Mountain Brewing Company
    (page 73)

Corrales

DRINKS

Ex Novo Brewing Company (page 78)

Albuquerque

EATS

66 Diner (page 17)
Albuquerque International Balloon Fiesta
    (page 116)
B2B Bistronomy (page 30)
Baca Boys Café (page 50)
The Candy Lady of Old Town (page 104)
Celina's Biscochitos (page 109)
Duran Central Pharmacy (pages 10
    and 122)
El Modelo Mexican Foods (page 122)
Eldora Craft Chocolate (page 104)
Frontier Restaurant (pages 17 and 122)
Golden Crown Panaderia (pages 105
    and 122)
Golden Pride BBQ, Chicken, and Ribs
    (page 11)
The Grill on San Mateo (page 31)
High Noon Restaurant and Saloon
    (pages 52 and 122)
Los Poblanos Historic Inn and Organic
    Farm (page 92)
Mary and Tito's Café (page 52)
Pop Fizz (page 105)
Pueblo Harvest (Indian Pueblo Kitchen),
    Indian Pueblo Cultural Center (page 107)
Range Café (pages 11 and 17)
Rebel Donut (page 105)
Rustic on the Green (page 31)

Sawmill Market (page 117)
Steel Bender Brewyard (page 31)
Ten 3, Sandiago's Grill at the Tram, Sandia
    Peak Tramway (page 117)
Tia Betty Blue's (page 122)
Twisters (page 12)
World Famous Laguna Burger (page 32)

DRINKS

Bosque Brewing Company (page 73)
Bow and Arrow Brewing Company
    (page 77)
Boxing Bear Brewing Company (page 73)
Broken Trail Spirits and Brew (page 91)
Canteen Brewhouse (page 77)
Casa Rondeña Winery (page 90)
Cutbow Coffee Roastery (page 113)
El Pinto Restaurant and Cantina
    (page 66)
Enchanted Circle Brewing (page 76)
Gruet Winery (page 91)
High Noon Restaurant and Saloon
    (page 66)
La Cumbre Brewing Company (page 74)
Left Turn Distilling (page 91)
Lescombes Winery and Bistro (page 92)
Los Poblanos Historic Inn and Organic
    Farm (page 92)
Marble Brewery (page 74)
New Mexico Piñon Coffee Café (page 113)
Nexus Restaurant, Taproom, Smokehouse
    (page 74)
Routes Bicycle Tours (page 116)
Safe House Distilling Company
    (page 91)
Santa Fe Brewing Company, Green Jeans
    Food Hall (page 31)
Sawmill Market (page 117)
Starr Brothers Brewing Company
    (page 74)
Still Spirits (page 91)
Toltec Brewing (page 75)
Tomasita's (pages 66 and 121)
Tractor Brewing Company
    (page 78)

Casa Blanca

EATS

Grandma Jo's Bakery (page 107)

Rio Puerco/Laguna

EATS

World Famous Laguna Burger (page 32)

Tucumcari

EATS

Kix on 66 (page 19)

Moriarty

DRINKS

Sierra Blanca Brewing Company (page 75)

Los Lunas

EATS

Range Café (pages 11 and 17)

DRINKS

Tractor Brewing Company (page 78)

Socorro

DRINKS

M Mountain Coffee House (page 113)

Pie Town

EATS

Pie-O-Neer Pies (page 106)

Portales

DRINKS

Roosevelt Brewing Company (page 81)

San Antonio

EATS

Buckhorn Tavern (page 33)

Owl Bar and Café (page 33)

Southern New Mexico

Truth or Consequences

DRINKS

Truth or Consequences Brewing Company (page 82)

Hatch

EATS

The Pepper Pot (page 20)

Sparky's Burgers, BBQ, and Espresso (pages 34 and 106)

Doña Ana

EATS

Chachi's Mexican Restaurant (page 35)

Las Cruces

EATS

Caliche's Frozen Custard (page 108)

Dick's Café (page 20)

Chachi's Mexican Restaurant (page 35)

Chala's Wood Fire Grill (page 35)

Habaneros Fresh Mex (page 55)

Las Cruces Farmers and Crafts Market (pages 109 and 118)

Osito's Biscochitos (page 109)

Pecan Grill and Brewery (page 123)

Santa Fe Grill, Pic Quik (page 13)

Si Señor Restaurant (pages 108 and 123)

DRINKS

Beck's Roasting House and Creamery (page 113)

The Bean Bakery Café (page 113)

Bosque Brewing Company (page 73)

D. H. Lescombes Winery and Las Cruces Bistro (pages 92 and 117)

Dry Point Distillery (page 93)

High Desert Brewing Company (page 78)

Icebox Brewing Company (page 79)

Little Toad Creek Brewery and Distillery (page 82)

Luna Rossa Winery (page 96)
Spotted Dog Brewery (page 79)
Truth or Consequences Brewing Company
  (page 82)

Mesilla

EATS

Legacy Pecans (page 108)
Peppers (page 35)
La Posta de Mesilla (page 55)

DRINKS

Imperial Bar, Double Eagle (page 67)
La Posta de Mesilla (page 55)
NM Vintage Wines Tasting Room
  (page 93)

La Mesa

EATS

Chope's Bar and Café (page 53)

Hillsboro

EATS

Hillsboro General Store Café (pages 36, 109,
  and 119)

DRINKS

Black Range Vineyards (pages 93
  and 119)

Silver City

EATS

Diane's Restaurant (pages 13 and 118)

DRINKS

La Esperanza Vineyard and Winery
  (Sherman) (pages 95 and 118)
Little Toad Creek Brewery and Distillery
  (pages 82 and 85)

Deming

EATS

Adobe Deli Onion Soup (page 123)

DRINKS

Lescombes Family Vineyards (page 96)
Luna Rossa Winery (page 96)

Columbus and Palomas, Mexico

DRINKS

The Pink Store (page 118)

Alamogordo

EATS

Caliche's Frozen Custard (page 108)
McGinn's Pistachioland (page 110)
Rockin' BZ Burgers (page 37)

DRINKS

Heart of the Desert Pistachios and Wine
  (page 96)
McGinn's Pistachioland (pages 96, 110,
  and 123)

Cloudcroft

EATS

Burro Street Bakery (page 110)
Eight the Cake (page 110)
KennaBelle's Kreations Bakery (page 110)
The Lodge Resort and Spa (page 119)
Mad Jack's Mountaintop Barbecue
  (pages 37 and 123)
Old Apple Barn (page 119)

DRINKS

Cloudcroft Brewing Company (page 83)
Noisy Water Winery (page 97)

Mescalero

EATS

Wendell's Steak and Seafood, Broken
  Arrow Taphouse, Inn of the Mountain
  Gods (pages 57 and 119)

Ruidoso

EATS

Club Gas (page 56)

Flying J Ranch (pages 57 and 119)
Hall of Flame Burgers (page 38)
Sacred Grounds Coffee and Tea House
(page 111)
Tina's Café (page 111)

DRINKS

Noisy Water Winery (page 97)

Glencoe

DRINKS

Glencoe Distillery (page 97)

Capitan

EATS

Oso Grill (page 39)

Lincoln

DRINKS

Bonito Valley Brewing Company
(page 83)

Roswell

EATS

Big D's Downtown Dive (page 20)
Chef Toddzilla's Gourmet Burgers and
Mobile Cuisine (page 41)

DRINKS

Antigua Cocina Mexicana (page 68)
Pecos Flavors Winery (page 97)
Peppers Grill and Bar (page 69)

Tatum

EATS

Steak House Café (page 123)

Lovington

EATS

Lazy 6 (page 111)

DRINKS

Drylands Brewing Company (page 83)

Artesia

DRINKS

Wellhead Restaurant and Brewpub
(page 83)

Carlsbad

EATS

Blue House Bakery and Café (page 112)
PJ & B Rio Café (page 13)

DRINKS

Guadalupe Mountain Brewing Company
(page 83)
Milton's Brewing (page 83)
The Trinity (page 98)

Acknowledgments

Whenever I told someone I was researching a book called *New Mexico Food Trails*, the response was always the same: "You have the best job!" They aren't wrong, but the travel and food writer life isn't always as glamorous as Instagram makes it look—and it requires a support crew that can provide an array of specialties.

Thankfully, I had such a crew, many of whom are foodies who didn't mind the grueling pace of driving and eating, ordering per my strict instructions, patiently posing their dishes in good light as I photographed them, sharing so that we could eat again at a place just up the road, and serving as designated drivers when needed. To that end, Danielle Burgess, thanks not only for your art direction but also your willingness to try avocado pie. And thanks to Heather Hunter, who not only provided a dose of "You got this" and marketing know-how but also jumped in the car at a moment's notice to drive to eateries with very unreliable hours. And thanks also for introducing me to Lore Dach, whose graphic design expertise keeps me and many others looking like pros.

To Liddie Martinez, author of *The Chile Line: Historic Northern New Mexico Recipes*, thanks for opening your farm and your heart to remind me that New Mexico's food heritage is about the people as much as it is about the chile.

I leaned heavily on my Albuquerque-based crew—Rob and Lisa, Todd and Elsie, Benton and Sara, Ken and Anaïs, Chris and Mel (and all of your kiddos)—who fed me tips and advice and, well, also just fed me, always knowing what I needed and when.

Every writer needs an editor, as well as someone to scoop them up off the floor when they lose all hope in their ability to craft a sentence. Christina Elston has always been the one to cut my fat and fix my words when they become a jumbled run-on. She also makes a mean batch of Christmas cookies. And to my rising-star fact-checker Kate Graham, thank you for pitching in and calling dozens of restaurant owners to make sure your weary mom didn't make too many embarrassing goofs.

To Sandy Short, my sister and partner in crime, thanks for your willingness to put diets aside for the sake of chocolate samplings and wine tastings, and for putting your arm around me when I inexplicably burst into tears at Smokey

Bear's gravesite in Capitan. And to Nancy and Chris, your words of encouragement (and swiftness at picking up the check) means more than you could ever know.

A huge wave of gratitude also goes to the crew at University of New Mexico Press for keeping me sharp and helping me bring this idea to fruition. Thanks also for getting me out into the state, where I got to eat some of the best meals of my life and meet some of the best people who made those meals.

And thank you, universe, for Steve Graham, who is always up for sharing a plate of enchiladas, sampling multiple craft brews, or researching an array of craft cocktails, even if it means driving from Farmington to Carlsbad. You along with our kiddos, Kate and Jackson, feed my soul and make all these adventures and accomplishments possible.

Index

About the Author

Carolyn Graham is a food and travel journalist, producer, and author who lives in Santa Fe. She has served as chief executive officer at *New Mexico Magazine* and editor in chief at *New Mexico Journey* (the AAA member publication) and has written about everything from pinto beans to Dolly Parton. She founded a production company and is creating a food culture and travel show packed with great stories about good eating and the people who make it happen. She was born in Las Cruces and has green chile in her blood: Her dad was raised nearby in Hatch, the green chile capital of the world, where her grandfather also ran Short's Café in the 1940s and '50s.

SOUTHWEST ADVENTURE SERIES
Ashley M. Biggers, Series Editor

The Southwest Adventure Series provides practical how-to guidebooks for readers seeking authentic outdoor and cultural excursions that highlight the unique landscapes of the American Southwest. Books in the series feature the best ecotourism adventures, world-class outdoor recreation sites, back-road points of interest, and culturally significant archaeological sites, as well as lead readers to the best sustainable accommodations and farm-to-table restaurants in Arizona, Colorado, Nevada, New Mexico, Utah, and Southern California.

Also available in the Southwest Adventure Series:

Arizona's Scenic Roads and Hikes: Unforgettable Journeys in the Grand Canyon State by Roger Naylor

Arizona State Parks: A Guide to Amazing Places in the Grand Canyon State by Roger Naylor

Eco-Travel New Mexico: 86 Natural Destinations, Green Hotels, and Sustainable Adventures by Ashley M. Biggers

Skiing New Mexico: A Guide to Snow Sports in the Land of Enchantment by Daniel Gibson